PICKING UP
THE PIECES

PICKING UP THE PIECES

*Finding Inner Peace
When Your World Falls Apart*

O. SONNY ACHO

CROSSWAY BOOKS • WHEATON, ILLINOIS
A DIVISION OF GOOD NEWS PUBLISHERS

Picking Up the Pieces

Copyright © 1996 by O. Sonny Acho, Ph.D.

Published by Crossway Books,
                a division of Good News Publishers
                1300 Crescent Street
                Wheaton, Illinois 60187.

Cover design: Cindy Kiple

Cover photo: Jim Whitmer

First printing 1996

Printed in the United States of America

Library of Congress Cataloging-in-Publication Data
Acho, O. Sonny, 1951-
   Picking up the pieces : finding inner peace when your world
falls apart/ O. Sonny Acho.
      p.   cm.
   Includes bibliographical references.
   ISBN 0-89107-913-0
   1. Consolation 2. Defeat (Psychology) 3. Christian life.
  I. Title.
  BV4905.2.A24   1996
  248.8'6—dc20   96-9880

04		03		02		01		00		99		98		97		96
15	14	13	12	11	10	9	8	7	6	5	4	3	2	1	

Dedicated to
my wife, Christie,
and my children—
Chiamaka, Stephanie, Samuel, and Emmanuel—
with gratitude for their sacrifice of time spent with me
in order that this book might be written

Contents

Acknowledgments

Special thanks to all those who have been willing to have me share experieces from their lives in this book. I would also like to thank Richard Greene and Sonia Jackson, whose editing skills helped to bring the material for this book to life.

Foreword

A great tension exists today between psychology and theology. On the one hand, there are those who write off all forms of psychotherapy as a satanically inspired deception causing people to depend on the flesh. On the other hand, there are those who imply that theology for the most part is an irrelevant discipline, though it may be helpful for those who have not been traumatized by life's tragic realities. This perspective marginalizes the Scriptures by simply using them to provide religious seasoning for what is essentially a secular approach to problem-solving.

In the middle of these two extremes stands my good friend and co-laborer, Sonny Acho. As Associate Pastor of Fellowship at Oak Cliff Bible Fellowship in Dallas, Dr. Acho has the challenging responsibility of overseeing our church's counseling ministry. He rightly recognizes that any true understanding of human nature, sin, personal responsibility, forgiveness, and restoration must be rooted in Scripture, the only absolute source of truth. However, he equally realizes that the trip from "isness" to "oughtness" is often traveled on a road paved with pain.

It is this reality that demands the presence of spiritually gifted men and women who not only can help, encourage, exhort, and direct those laboring under life's burdens, but who also can train others to do likewise.

This is the unique and strategic role of the professional Christian counselor today. They must lead those whose worlds have fallen apart to locate the broken pieces of their lives and begin putting them back together again. This is neither an insignificant nor small task. It is, in fact, one of the primary roles of the local church. It is precisely because Christians find it so difficult to recognize and analyze the source of their brokenness that there is the need for the Christian community, under the guidance of spiritually gifted, biblically saturated counselors, to help the body to fulfill its God-given task of encouraging and restoring one another. In addition, godly counselors can fill the vital role of providing an alternative to the godless secular approaches to counseling that abound today.

In this fine work, Dr. Acho shows why and how Christian counseling, properly done, helps people pick up the pieces of their broken lives in such a way that Scripture is honored, the Holy Spirit is utilized, Christ is glorified, God is obeyed, and people are helped.

Whether you are a person whose world has been shattered or a person who is helping a loved one pick up life's pieces, this book will help you understand that there is no pit so deep that God is not deeper still.

—*Tony Evans*

Preface

Over the years, my outlook on Christian counseling has undergone a vast transformation. This transformation occurred when my idealism about ministry in Christian counseling met with reality.

Upon completion of my doctorate degree, I had a growing desire to use my training and gift for counseling in a Christian organization. My particular desire to serve in that setting was fueled by my yearning to minister to believers who were having difficulty experiencing the full effect of their salvation. Paul's admonition in Romans 15:1 for the strong to help those who are weak was definite motivation for my desire to practice in a way that edified the household of God.

In pursuit of my desire, I became a therapist in a Christian counseling organization. My new position in the hospital afforded me the opportunity to practice a Christ-centered approach to mental health and healing. Biblical principles were the basis for psychological analysis, in keeping with both my training and desire.

I expected the majority of my patients to be newcomers to the faith who, for some reason, were not able to maximize their new life in Christ. Most likely they would still be wrestling with the vestiges of their former lives. I thought that my greatest task was going to be simply to guide them toward a deeper relationship with Christ. I anticipated having to counsel those who had heard and received the Gospel but who could not realize the ramifications of a renewed life in the Savior. I believed my main purpose as a counselor in this new setting would be to provide assistance to those who were struggling by helping them understand themselves and become strong in the Word of God.

However, to my amazement, that was not the case. I was surprised at the number of patients who knew Christ and knew the right things to do, but who were experiencing conflict in their daily walk with Him. People who had been Christians for ten years, twenty years, and longer were admitting themselves into the hospital for treatment. Patients were coming from across the nation to this facility with their struggles and their conflicts in search of a biblically based solution. They came to the facility as the Israelites in Exodus 18 went to Moses to learn the statutes of God and His laws when they had a dispute with others or experienced conflict within themselves.

In my daily practice, I saw not only babes in Christ who were struggling with pain, but also those who had been believers for quite some time. I asked myself, "How can these things be?" The reality that I faced was not what I had envisioned. Many of the patients who checked themselves into the hospital had a relationship with Christ. They knew about the cross, the sufficiency of Christ, the Word of God, and God's biblical instructions for life. My past and current clients searching for help include ministers of large congregations, seminary students who have devoted significant portions of their lives to the study of Scripture, and lay leaders who have committed themselves to a life of service.

The patients of the past, the patients of the present, and the patients of the future all have struggles uniquely theirs, but their struggles have something in common. The common cord that binds the predicaments of so many patients is the destructive tension between the real and the ideal—the ideal of a new and abundant life in Christ versus the reality of our painful existence on earth.

Even though we know we are sinners who can only receive justification before God through Jesus Christ, even though we are aware of the power of the Holy Spirit to guide and help us through the trials of life, and even though we realize the importance of fellowship with other believers, the fact is that what we expect in our Christian life is not always what we experience. What we hope for does not always happen, and what we anticipate is not always actualized. This is a reality of life, and this reality causes pain. Many try to dodge the hurt and hide the pain behind a religious facade, Christian cliches, or excessive church service. Others turn to addictive behaviors in order to abate the misery resident in the recesses of their hearts and minds.

I have seen that the initial struggle these patients endure is complicated by guilt when Christians from their pulpits and/or their books condemn them for seeking counseling, dismissing the emotional results of their struggle as simple weakness or sin.

A misrepresentation has been accepted by many believers—the idea that all psychologists, even those who base their practice on the Word of God, are evil agents seeking to destroy the lordship of Christ over our lives. Many well-known pastors warn their members not to seek biblically based counseling. Physical sickness is accepted in their church members; visits are even made to the hospital when someone has been admitted for surgery or other illness. Spiritually sick people are also accepted in the gathering of believers, and an invitation to accept Jesus Christ as their Lord and Savior is extended to them at the close of the message or during some other time in the worship service. In addition, churches organize evangelistic outreaches in which spiritually sick, or unsaved, people are sought out in order to extend to them the healing that Christ offers. Christians who are suffering emotionally, however, are dismissed as "weak" or simply needing to "trust in the Lord." Neither relevance nor remedy is given to their pain by platitudes. Their conflict is real, their battle against evil angels and principalities is real, and the repeated defeat they experience causes inner turmoil.

It is that conflict I desire to address. I want to speak to the pain that occurs when what people believe conflicts with what they experience—when people know the outcome they want, they do what they believe they need to do to get it, but the results are far from what they had expected. I will address the mess that occurs when people hear the Word on Sunday, but when the rubber meets the road on Monday, the crash occurs, and the pieces of their lives become a puzzle. This book is written as a support for those whose world has been shattered, to encourage them as they begin picking up the pieces.

Part One

Observing the Puzzle

One

Our Worlds: Have They Been Shattered?

Have you ever heard the expression, "My whole world is falling apart"? What do people mean by this? Certainly they are not saying that the planet is undergoing some seismic or galactic disturbance. The "whole world" in this familiar phrase represents the network of relationships any individual maintains with family, friends, and others.

These relationships have much to do with a person's values, goals, perspectives, and self-esteem. Relationships are what makes everyone's "world go 'round." Relationships are also what makes everyone's world come to a screeching halt. This paradox sounds similar to the opening of Dickens's *A Tale of Two Cities:* "It was the best of times; it was the worst of times." Dickens's classic statement might easily describe most relationships.

The world of relationships can supply many wonderful moments of joy, as when two young parents share in the birth of their first child or when a father tosses the baseball to his son in the backyard. Conversely, relationships can become frightening, disharmonious, and disrupting. The idea of dreadful relationships conjures up pictures of spouse abuse, child abuse, or the stress caused by a teenager's supposedly complete and unblemished understanding of how the world works, over and against the relatively experienced and informed views of his or her parents.

It is truly mind-boggling how one thing could be both good and horrible at the same time. James 3:11-12 asks, "Can both fresh water and salt water flow from the same spring? My brothers, can a fig tree bear olives, or a grapevine bear figs? Neither can a salt spring produce fresh water." The questions James asks are rhetorical. He suggests that the two results are mutually exclusive. The question requires a "no" answer.

In my own tenure as a counselor, I have personally witnessed inconsistencies such as those James mentions. I have seen marriages that involve passionate lovemaking, and in the very next moment disintegrate into heated arguments, infidelity, and even physical violence. Similarly, I have seen fathers who were immensely proud of a son's or daughter's accomplishments. Yet these same fathers can turn around and sexually, verbally, or mentally abuse these children. Throughout my career, I have seen situations like these; even so, somehow I am gripped with a sense of bewilderment and awe.

Jane, a twenty-five-year-old accountant in a large established firm, came to me when she started experiencing confusion as to what to think or how to feel about her relationship with her spouse, whom she dearly loved. She had been married for two years to her college sweetheart and was four months pregnant when she came to my office.

Jane was attempting to understand why her husband would express what she believed was true love, but at the same time he would be angry with her to the point of pushing, hitting, and attempting to strangle her on a regular basis. Her husband would come home from work complaining that the house was in a mess, and an argument would erupt. The argument would lead to pushing. Her husband would get in a rage over a dirty plate in the sink. Jane said, "He always finds something to fuss about, but by the same token, he wants to be close to me on a regular basis, and he constantly tells me that he loves me."

Jane went on to say that she knew her husband loved her dearly and that she loved him very much as well, but she just wanted the physical abuse to stop. Jane's family and friends had advised her to leave her husband. Her response was to deny any real problem, saying that her husband was merely "going through a phase." But in a very real sense, Jane's world had shattered. She was confused and desperately needed guidance.

Victoria was sixteen years old when her mother brought her to my office in bewilderment. You see, Victoria's mother had remarried when the girl was two years old. Victoria's stepfather was the only father she had known. He was the man who raised her, but all of a sudden, at age fifteen, Victoria said that her stepfather had started making uncomfortable sexual remarks when they were alone. That led to hugging her regularly, which eventually led to having sex with her. Victoria, of course, like other children, wondered what she might have done to cause the sexual abuse. Because of guilt and fear of being blamed and, most of all, of losing the only father she had ever known, Victoria could not tell anybody until her pregnancy at age sixteen forced her to share this horrible shattered relationship with her mother. I remember Victoria asking how a stepfather who truly loved her all those years could yet hurt her as he did. She was shocked by the reality that people can hurt and cause pain to those they love. What these two women did not understand is that every individual has the ability to love and to hurt, and a person can move from one to the other, depending on what is happening in his or her life at a particular time.

Unfortunately, the world of relationships is a fallen world, a world that is "void and without form," where darkness rules. This darkness is a haven for all sorts of disorderly and sinister desires that fiendishly lurk in the hidden places of the heart—arrogance, ungratefulness, treachery, selfishness, conceit, and brutality. These things shatter and disrupt the relationships people try to maintain.

Fortunately, this scenario was not at all the design of the Master Architect. Human relationships were intended to be blissful and complete, with positive interaction between people. Relationships were to make up our Garden of Eden, but somehow they have become vineyards for wayward weeds and thistles. Given the choice between Eden and a weed nursery, few people, if any, would choose weeds. Unfortunately, because everyone is part of a fallen world, the weeds are what everyone inherits. If babies only knew what type of world they were coming into, I suppose many of them would fight to remain in the womb.

No one possesses a natural immunity to dysfunctional relationships; no family has cornered the market on perfection; no teacher can educate away the problems we humans have relating to one another; no religion can guarantee a perfect world without any cracks in it. Not even Christians are immune to poor relationships. They are subject to the same relational and emotional maladies as anyone else. If this seems odd, consider some of the comments in the apostle Paul's epistles. First Corinthians 1:10-11 reads: "I appeal to you, brothers, in the name of our Lord Jesus Christ, that all of you agree with one another so that there may be no divisions among you and that you may be perfectly united in mind and thought. My brothers, some from Chloe's household have informed me that there are quarrels among you." This statement comes from a letter to a church, a community of love, but there was quarreling and bickering among the ranks. Philippians 4:1 states, "I plead with Euodia and I plead with Syntyche to agree with each other in the Lord." But it gets worse. Not only was there bickering but also incest. First Corinthians 5:1 says: "It is actually reported that there is sexual immorality among you, and of a kind that does not occur even among pagans: A man has his father's wife." Twenty centuries ago the apostle Paul faced the same dilemmas that pastors and counselors face today.

The basic nature of people has not changed in over two thousand years. Christians are human too and are therefore subject to the same predicaments as everyone else. What should be different is the Christian's ability to handle difficult situations. However, because of a lack of growth, tremors and quakes (emanating from the past and the present) cause cracks in our lives and in our worlds. Relational problems are like earthquakes. An earthquake may initially be one violent event, but the ruin caused by aftershocks and structural damage continues. Faulty attempts to repair damage caused by quakes and tremors can exacerbate the problem. This is especially true when we use temporary quick fixes to try to repair long-term damage.

The Quick-Fix Syndrome

Many social and spiritual problems harm our society. So many that if every one of them were written down, I suppose that even the whole world would not have room for the books that would be written. In my estimation, the number one societal malignancy is the tendency to apply quick fixes to long-term problems.

The "quick-fix syndrome," the idea that faster is better, inundates our culture. Everyone feels the need for speed and seeks the path of least resistance. The advertising world does a wonderful job of exploiting this tendency and tries its best to perpetuate this myth (or lifestyle or mind-set). Diet pills promise overnight miracles that change men from human hamburgers to Hercules and women to Venus de Milo. Forget about the simple idea of eating wholesome foods with less fat and exercising for thirty minutes three times a week. That takes too long. Fast-food restaurants say you deserve a break and entice you to come in and buy one of their high-calorie, low-nutrition cholesterol-makers. Hey, it's fast and it's easy. Then there are those commercials that advocate avoiding college in favor of pursuing a career as a "nail technician." Obtain a five-week degree from Good Ole Finger Tech. Not that anything is wrong with honest work, but a college degree has certain advantages. And rightly so, considering the required time and discipline that go into acquiring one.

Advertising is not alone in this emphasis on Band-Aid remedies. The government covers social and fiscal problems with ad hoc legislation and tax increases. If deemed necessary, more money is printed—a process that does not solve any dilemma but makes everyone happy for a little while—that is, until the next judgment day (April 15). Computer manufacturers boast of 150-megahertz chips processing at a speed faster than 133-megahertz chips when, in actuality, the user detects virtually no difference .

Nevertheless, someone has to have the newer machine because it's faster. Have you noticed the proliferation of "paid programming" in the television guide? You know, those dreadful hour-long commercials, some of which tell you how to become independently wealthy through buying real estate with no capital. The stock market, too, has fallen victim to the pursuit of the quick and easy. Companies have difficulty achieving long-range goals because of the American investor's penchant for profit. "Here's my $50. Turn it into $100 by tomorrow or I will divest!" The propagation of quick fixes also affects our kitchens; supermarkets now provide the ability to microwave a whole meal. Let's face it, the old conventional slow-but-sure methodology is a thing of the past.

This microwave mentality carries over into relationships. The quick fix for marriage is divorce. Never mind renovating that deteriorating marriage; get a girlfriend or a boyfriend. The quick-fix solution for children is called "ignore them"; for parents, it's "Don't call me and I won't call you—until I need something." The quick fix for the inconvenience of the elderly is the nursing home. Then there is the most heinous quick fix of all, the substitution of churchgoing for a real, genuine, true, life-changing, and life-producing relationship with God—esteeming two hours in church on Sunday as better than making the other six days and twenty-two hours a time of prayer and devotion. We don't have the patience and perseverance to "pray without ceasing" (1 Thessalonians 5:17 KJV).

Seemingly, nothing is so sacred as to be safe from the quick-fix syndrome. Relationships, weight loss, food—you name it—no one and nothing is immune to its influence, not even Christians! Few people desire the fire of an authentic relationship with God, true zest in their lives. Because real fire takes time, most people just want to be heated up for the moment. People seek microwave solutions to their relational problems when those problems really need to be slow roasted.

Our individual worlds consist of the relationships we maintain or tolerate. Relationships have much to do with how we feel and what we become. When a relationship goes awry, the human tendency is to seek out other avenues for fulfillment rather than buckle down and deal with the problem.

Just Deal with It

The net effect of the microwave mentality translates into coping with problems rather than resolving them. There is a time to apply a strong coping mechanism while waiting on God, and there is a time to apply faith and hope as one takes action. Of course, a certain kind of coping can be responsible and appropriate. The coping that psychologists encourage is the ability to wait patiently. Coping can, however, become a pacifier. It does not provide long-term solutions for problem areas. Pacifiers are meant for a certain stage in an infant's life, and babies eventually outgrow them. At a certain stage in a crisis, coping is appropriate. However, the time comes when healing must take place.

Adults who continue to rely on pacifiers instead of exchanging them for the "meat" that provides healing will not solve any of their problems. The truth is that when babies become adults, they often merely change pacifiers. Adult pacifiers are much more sophisticated and much harder to outgrow than baby pacifiers.

What I've observed over the years are people who, because of fear, have difficulty making a decision to go to the next step. We see many husbands who remain stagnant in a sick relationship, reluctant to move forward because of fear.

A few weeks ago, I had the privilege of performing a wedding where I encouraged the groom not to be afraid of dealing with any issues that may arise in his relationship. I referred the couple to Genesis 2:19, which tells how God formed every beast of the field and every bird of the sky and asked Adam to move forward by naming them. In chapter 3 Adam refused to take charge when the serpent visited the garden. Several books have been written on Adam and where he was during that conversation.

Since the Bible didn't say he left the garden, I believe Adam was right there with his wife. It is obvious from Eve's conversation with the serpent that she enjoyed talking. Maybe Adam didn't take to her talkativeness and therefore chose not to deal with it. Had he dealt with the serpent himself, Eve wouldn't have been tricked.

Most relationships are like Adam and Eve's. Most people know what is going on but will choose not to face it for different reasons.

One reason may be fear of saying something that will make matters worse. *He or she may be angry at finding out I feel this way. He or she may leave or get a divorce.* Another reason may be the fear of being viewed negatively. For example: *I've always maintained a Mr. Nice Guy image and would like very much to keep it that way.*

One of the first questions I ask couples who come to my office with marital problems is: "How long have you been having this problem?"

Often they will say, "Since we have been married."

I then ask, "How long have you been married?"

Some say ten years or so, and I come to find out that they have been struggling because they've refused to face the problem. I understand that they have not been honest with one another because of fear of what the partner may say or think.

They are also dishonest with other people. Ask them how they are doing, and you will hear something like "very good, very close, relating well, understanding each other, communicating well," etc., while the fact remains that they don't really know each other well. How could a person claim to know someone yet never share true feelings or burdens with that person?

A few years ago, I had a client who saw me about every week for six months without honestly sharing what brought her to my office. I sensed that what she was telling me during six months of therapy was not what really had caused her to seek counseling. We dealt with what she presented and a few other side issues, until one day during the seventh month, she decided to share the real deal.

"Why did it take you this long?" I asked.

She responded, "I wanted so bad for you to accept me, not reject me nor judge me, because everybody has when I've been honest with them."

So she was assuming that because some people she had been

close to had judged her, I would judge her also. Of course, when I asked specifically how many people she was referring to as "everybody," she couldn't count more than four. So in her mind, four persons means everybody. It is interesting to see the projection that took place. This woman met me without getting to know me and projected on me what a few people had done to her. What this woman did to me, we often do to each other.

People mistreat us in relationships or on the job. We refuse to deal with it or express our feelings about it and just conclude in our own minds that's how everybody is. In similar situations with somebody else, we would surely receive the same treatment. But that is a false way of thinking. I'm sure if you were married before and your spouse cheated on you, you feel apprehensive when approached again for marriage. Though your feelings may be legitimate or normal, they should not translate into a belief that the next spouse will treat you exactly the same way. We must learn how to ask questions about something we're unsure of and stop making false assumptions—thinking the problem will go away if we ignore it.

The attitude of coping rather than conquering never allows the individual to grow and mature in the faith. The result is lifelong denial versus living in the light of truth and reality. The quick fix is the only solution for people who feel they cannot change. For the Christian, the quick fix is not a viable alternative. God is able to change what may very well seem unchangeable to us (Ephesians 3:20).

To add insult to injury, the problem with merely tolerating deep-seated problems is that complications develop. First, the individual never gains any true sense of accomplishment. Second, he or she never learns how to confront problems head-on. The third and perhaps worst side effect of all is that the individual spirals more deeply and painfully into depression and agony.

Once pain enters the cycle again, avoiding that pain becomes the major goal in the person's life. All her life Lisa had attended a church with strong biblical teaching that discouraged divorce. Her husband never indicated that anything was wrong with their marriage of thirty years until he informed her he was having an affair. She survived the initial shock. But because she could not accept that a marriage of thirty years was about to end in divorce and could not deal with the shame, fear, or embarrassment, she decided to avoid the pain. First, she asked her husband to come over at least three times a week for sexual relations. Second, she encouraged him not to discuss the separation and pending divorce with anyone, including family members and people on her job, with the exception of talking to me in our counseling sessions. Third, Lisa would call her husband and tell him not to feel guilty about what he had done, but rather to go on with his life as if nothing had happened.

One and a half years passed after her husband had been gone and had filed for divorce. He got a job two hundred miles away from Lisa. To avoid dealing with the pain of divorce, Lisa requested that her husband allow her to visit him in the city there. I had to confront her. Of course, Lisa denied behaving in such a manner—until we went through all her attempts one by one. Lisa's behavior was a clear indication that she didn't want to deal with reality, but rather planned to avoid the pain that comes with broken relationships.

Every broken relationship carries its consequences, whether it is a one-week relationship or a thirty-year marriage relationship. In either one, the pain usually may be associated with some brokenness in an individual's relationships during childhood. Of course, any pain one chooses to avoid dealing with will only surface again later. Such avoidance is not productive. It is a retreat! The constant mode of retreat leaves the individual in a relentless whirlwind of helplessness. Paul echoes this horrendous sense of defeat when he says, "But I see another law at work in the members of my body, waging war against the law of my mind and making me a prisoner of the law of sin at work within my members" (Romans 7:23).

Romans 7:23 is the sound of a soul in turmoil. A deep yearning resides in the heart to become a true example of the workmanship of God; however, the pain produced by sin and our own unwillingness to solve our problems in God's way hammer away at our world, cracking and shattering all those relationships designed to help make us healthy and sound people of God.

In a 1960s movie called *Crack in the Earth*, some scientists had the not-so-bright idea that if they punched a hole in the crust of the earth, they could tap the geothermal energy of the earth's core. There was only one tiny problem. The scientists did not realize that once they punched the hole, the hot, molten material from the earth's core would began to eat through the crust. This small hole precipitated an irreversible chain of events; the acidic erosion circumnavigated the earth, resulting in the earth splitting in half. What was designed to be a complete and perfect whole now became two useless pieces of a planet. The scientists did everything they could to stop the crack. For every move they made, the crack made a counter move. The end result was that a large portion of the earth was hurled into space.

Whatever is devastating and eating away at your world God really wants to fix. However, if the crack is to stop before your whole world falls apart, then God alone has to do it. The more you try in your own strength, the more you will fail; and the more you fail, the more you will hurt.

A couple that had been married for fifteen years came to me with much pain over the wife's desire to divorce the husband. I asked him, "Why does your wife want the divorce?" He said that for the past fourteen years he had been in and out of work and had not financially provided for her. He also said he had had a couple of affairs and had been physically abusive a few times. He went on to share how in the last year things had changed. He was now with a great company, made good money, had not been involved with any other women, had not hit her, went to church regularly, bought her flowers frequently, and continued working to do more. Having done all of that over the last year and considering all that he planned to do in the future, he couldn't understand why it was not enough to stop her from pursuing the divorce. His inability to make his wife feel differently was beginning to bother him.

What he seemed to forget is that emotional wounds are very different from physical wounds. A physician friend who specializes in surgery once said to me that he would never be a good counselor. When dealing with or trying to help people recover from emotional pain, he found it difficult because there was nothing he could see or operate on and watch heal. He described emotional problems as a big onion with many layers, with each layer carrying a lot of complicated, unseen bad feelings. He was trying to say that emotional wounds take time to heal.

I tell my practicum students that what a client brings to the session initially may be just the presenting problem and not what is really going on with them. A wife may distrust the husband, not because of what he just did, but because she has not dealt with the fact that the husband, prior to marrying her, was cheating on his ex-wife with her. A thirty-four-year-old woman whom I treated for major depression blamed her condition on the fact that while married, she was attracted to a twenty-nine-year-old well-to-do professional man and started having an affair. As the affair progressed, out of guilt at deceiving her husband, she divorced him and married the twenty-nine-year-old man.

Six years later, she and her new husband showed up in my office wanting a divorce. The first thing that came out of her husband's mouth during the initial interview was, "I couldn't live with the guilt anymore. For six years I've been living a lie and attempting to make sense out of our behavior, and I can't." The woman, who was having problems getting pregnant, blamed those problems on her affair. The guilt created sexual difficulties and relational problems with her present husband. Needless to say, nothing that the present husband did was good enough, because she was still living with their past mistake and wrong choices.

Of course, the task of getting them to let go of the past and move forward wasn't easy. I pointed out to the man that there are some mistakes we are not able to undo and that this might be one of them. I encouraged him to consider allowing God to change his wife's feelings as he continued doing positive things for the relationship.

As the apostle Paul realized in Romans 7, it is Jesus Christ and Him alone who can mend the failed relationships all people have—both with God and with other men and women. "What a wretched man I am! Who will rescue me from this body of death? Thanks be to God—through Jesus Christ our Lord" (Romans 7:24-25a). The Father's original design did not include the broken, shattered lives so many experience. He created us to be whole, perfect beings, fully pleasing to Him. Healing can begin as we understand who He designed us to be.

Two

The Once-Perfect Puzzle: The Original Design

In order to progress toward the healing of a shattered life, one must examine God's original design for human beings. It is not until we explore His initial intentions that we are fully able to grasp the extent of the destruction that has occurred. After we have analyzed our situation in relation to His intended purpose, we are able to define the strategy for assembling the pieces.

Genesis 1:27 testifies that God made men and women in His own image. If we have been created in the image of God, it is only natural that we should ask, "What is the image of God?" and "What should we do to bear His image properly?"

To begin to answer these questions, we must understand several things. The Bible states that the creation of man combined both the physical and the spiritual into one being. Adam was made from the dust of the earth (Genesis 2:7)—a feature in common with the environment over which he reigned. However, the breath of life, which quickened his spirit, came from God. Man's physical nature was an aspect in common with the universe, but his spiritual nature was exclusive. God reserved His breath of life for human beings alone. So then, what did God create when He made the human race?

In bringing man into existence, God created a very special being. Psalm 8:5 tells us that He made man a "little lower than the heavenly beings and crowned him with glory and honor." God crowns us above all the rest of His creation. We have been made rulers over all God's creation. Our dominion extends not only to things living but to all things, including our circumstances. The Bible teaches us that "the earth is the Lord's and the fullness thereof." In other words, God has designed us to be in control of our circumstances, not under them. God's plans for us are a lot greater than many of us realize.

In view of God's wonderful purpose for humankind, what has happened to us? Why do we live under our circumstances rather than above them? Why do we not live up to our potential as recipients of such crowning glory and honor?

Scripture also tells us we are "fearfully and wonderfully made" (Psalm 139:14). Our value is far above the value of any other thing God has made. A combination of both material and immaterial substance enabled Adam to relate to both the environment in which he lived and to the glorious God who made him. By divine assignment, human beings have the responsibility to control the world that God established, just as God reigns over all that is.

In order for us to exercise our dominion properly according to God's design, we must be able to relate well to others. The most important aspect of our role as God's image-bearers is our desire for association—with our God first, and then with others. Of course, one of my reasons for writing this book is to deal with our inability to relate well to one another. The majority of people who suffer from depression will tell you that their condition stems from relational problems. Most of the suicide attempts by young and old people each year result from a breakdown in relationships. Today our jails are full of people who got into trouble through violating the laws that govern how we relate to one another.

We get into all these difficulties because we have mistaken ideas about how relationships should function. We refuse to let the Scriptures define for us what relationships are to be. When the Bible speaks of marriage in Ephesians 5, it explains clearly why God brings a man and a woman together as husband and wife. I see Paul saying that the purpose for marriage is that the couple demonstrate to the unsaved world what the relationship between Christ and His church is like. Sexual gratification is a blessing that attends that relationship. Children are a blessing of the marriage, but they should not be the primary goal of the union.

After being married for nine years, Scott decided to get a divorce because he wanted a child, and his wife could not give him one. Two years into his marriage, Scott's wife had said, "Honey, I am having some health problems and need to have surgery done that might remove my reproductive system."

Scott said, "No problem. You have my support."

Well, the support lasted only a few months after the surgery. Scott decided he was not going to be God's image-bearer in his marital relationship. Later his unhappiness led to dissatisfaction, withdrawal, and then divorce, which left his wife with a shattered world. It seems that Scott was only able to relate when he was getting or hoped to get what he wanted out of the relationship. When his expectations could no longer be realized, selfishness set in. The marriage vows and the commitment to be there in sickness and in health became null and void.

We relate to God primarily through prayer, and He relates to us through the holy Scriptures. We relate to one another through verbal and physical communication. Man was created to be a relater, just as God is a relater.

The age-old question, "Who is God?" often spurs long and lofty discourses as people attempt philosophically to define His essence or being. We as Christians, on the other hand, are urged to demonstrate the nature of our heavenly Father by concrete actions that capture His identity in one sentence—God is love. This gives us the opportunity to share the beauty of relationships implicit in His creative design.

Consider the Trinity—the Father, Son, and Holy Spirit—and how they exist as a community of one. Why would God, who is omnipotent, omniscient, and omnipresent, use three personalities to demonstrate His character? What characteristics would three persons illustrate that one spiritual being could not?

It is obvious that God can choose whatever means He desires to communicate to His children. So God exhibited Himself in the person of the Father, the Son, and the Holy Spirit to model His love—a love whose demonstration and expression require a relationship. There are many things one person can do alone, but loving is not one of them. Love, by design, was intended to be shared with someone else. People who love only themselves are unhealthy. In the act of love, one must give and one must receive. Throughout Scripture, the transfer of love is always accomplished within the context of relationships. In 2 Samuel 9 we find this demonstrated in the relationship David had with Jonathan.

David and Jonathan had a unique friendship. Their relationship could best be described as covenantal. Their loyalty toward each other was so strong that it even extended long after Jonathan had died. In this passage, we find David asking one of his servants, Ziba, "Is there anyone still left of the house of Saul to whom I can show kindness for Jonathan's sake?" Why would David seek out someone in Jonathan's family to whom he could show kindness? Wasn't it Jonathan's father Saul who had tried for twelve years to kill David? You would think that the family of someone who wanted him dead would be the last place he would look for someone to be kind to.

To fully understand David's motives, we have to appreciate the bond that existed between David and Jonathan (1 Samuel 20:14-17). Remembering the depth of their relationship, David sought out Jonathan's grandson Mephibosheth, who had been lame since he was five, and welcomed him into his household as if he were one of David's own sons. It was out of the context of David and Jonathan's friendship that Mephibosheth received this kind and loving act from David.

The Trinity provides a perfect example of a healthy relationship. Their association is marked by unconditional love. God the Father, God the Son, and God the Holy Spirit do not compete with one another. Neither do they demonstrate selfishness in their relationship, as we do. The Spirit does not envy the glorified position of the Son. The Son does not boast of His deity and rebel against the Father. Though that harmony once existed in the context of human relationships, it was lost in the Garden of Eden. As a result, disharmony has characterized human relationships ever since.

Consider Cain and Abel. A harmonious relationship between the two brothers was ruined when Cain became jealous because Abel's sacrifice was more acceptable to God than Cain's (Genesis 4:1-8). Scripture is threaded with such relationships: Saul's jealousy when the people praised David for killing Goliath (1 Samuel 18:6-11) and Paul splitting with Barnabas over the inclusion of Mark in the missionary party (Acts 15:36-40).

Though the initial harmony among men and women was interrupted, the harmonious alliance among the members of the Trinity is eternal. There is never an argument among them. Each is equal in essence, and each respects and supports the role of the other. We say in psychology that respect is what you have to have in order to get it. A lot of us have problems respecting ourselves and, as a result, have difficulty extending it to others.

I was raised in a community in Africa where every person wants to be number one. That same spirit jeopardizes the unity of most nations in Africa. For example, in Nigeria the Ibo tribe, the Hausa in the northern part of the country, and the Yorubas in the west all want to be number one. The military says they are the most important and can best rule the nation. The civilians say they are number one and need to be in power. Show me a nation with such a mentality, and I will show you a nation full of chaos, strife, jealousy, and envy. Of course, with such a spirit also comes a lack of productivity as well as confusion.

When I was a child, my father at Christmastime would send my clothes to be made by a tailor who was being trained by my father's tailor. One Christmas this young trainee, who had only been an apprentice for nine months, convinced my father that he had become a master tailor. After a few months, he was going to sew my clothes by himself without his master's input. Needless to say, when we picked up my shirt and trousers on December 24th and I tried them on, the trousers were tight and the shirt was too big. Because it was Christmas Eve, and all the tailors had gone to their villages to celebrate Christmas, nothing could be done. I still remember how miserable I was as a ten-year-old boy on that Christmas morning. I cried almost all day and refused to be comforted. Most families function like that tailor, each member thinking he or she knows it all, refusing to allow another member who might be more knowledgeable about a subject to give advice or handle it.

Often couples start disrespecting each other's roles. For example, a wife gets angry because her husband has been called by God to be a leader, and she won't let him lead, or the men become jealous of the wife's position in the family. Confused messages are sent to the children. Both spouses will be unhappy and will accomplish nothing as a team. With this mentality, relationships become a competitive endeavor, as opposed to a complementary endeavor—the perfect picture of harmony.

Through the relationship of the three persons of the Trinity, God is able to fulfill His design. God by His very threefold nature is a relater. He is three divine persons in one being, having one holy essence, and after His own design, He made men and women. God placed so much care and genius into the creation of human beings that it stifles the imagination.

Yet, before God all people are like grass. They spring up, and then they dry up and die. However, God still cares for this most fickle creature called man. Throughout the annals of history, many have wondered why, including the great men of the Scriptures. In Psalm 8:3-6, David rehearsed the majesty and splendor of God. In the process, the thought occurred to him: Since God is so wonderful, and since His name is so majestic in all the earth, why in the world does He care about mere men? "When I consider your heavens, the work of your fingers, the moon and the stars, which you have set in place, what is man that you are mindful of him, the son of man that you care for him? You made him a little lower than the heavenly beings and crowned him with glory and honor. You made him ruler over the works of your hands; you put everything under his feet." As David thought about all the things God has done for man, he was utterly amazed and overcome with praise to God.

This wonderful plan for human beings described in the psalm is typical of what our heavenly Father does for His children. For God, none of this is out of the ordinary. Our life is intended to be a fulfilling enterprise of fruitful labor—not because the work itself is fulfilling, but because of the relationship with the One who assigned the work.

Life was designed to be lived in concert with God. Only one who is in fellowship with the Lord can truly know His immense love and, in turn, truly love others. People in and of themselves can't love because they don't understand love. In most cases, people have a selfish love—a love based on what someone has done for them lately or on the ways they benefit from the relationship.

It's amazing how many people come to me saying that their spouse doesn't mop the floor regularly or doesn't cut the grass often or doesn't get up early enough in the morning. These failures make it impossible to care for the spouse anymore. I always ask if they mean that they stopped loving because of what the other is not doing. The reply will often be: "How can you love a person who doesn't do what's expected of them?" In other words, our love is based on works.

I've seen spouses who say, "The question we need to answer is: Is it possible to love and do those things that demonstrate love when my spouse is not behaving positively?" Is it fair to ask someone to love you in spite of your behavior? Even though it is biblical to love in spite of what someone does, I will submit that it is difficult to do. Only when we have received and understood the love of God are we able to love and relate with others God's way.

God designed us to be secure and trusting creatures who dwell in the paradise of life inside nurturing relationships. Relationship is the means by which we are to experience fulfillment. As obstacles arise, our ability to experience fulfilled relations breaks down. But we are not designed to live in isolation. God said, "It is not good for man to be alone" (Genesis 2:18). As image-bearers, we must learn to look to God for the definition and embodiment of relationship. We must understand that relationship begins with God; therefore, our focus must be the biblical guidelines for association with our families, friends, and others in the household of faith. Whether we edify or degrade, nurture or neglect, we relate with others. This interaction begins early in life. The results remain for the rest of our lives.

We have already established that how we interact as adults

largely depends on how we were raised. If one received a lot of nurture, it is easier for that person to nurture as an adult. If one was hurt, he or she has a tendency to hurt others also. If one was raised in a family where laughter came easily, that person will likely laugh much and share good humor with other people. We really can't say enough about the need for positive parenting. Sad to say, everything in our society suggests that we either don't care enough or don't understand the impact we have on our young people.

When I was growing up, there wasn't a lot of hugging around our house. Daddy didn't hug Mom. Mom didn't hug Daddy. The children didn't receive hugs from the parents either. As an adult, I decided I was going to show open affection to my wife and children. Because of the decision I made as an adult, I easily give and receive hugs and affection from my wife and children. But it is a struggle to be affectionate to my mom. When she comes to visit or when I go home, I plan beforehand not only to give her a hug when I first see her but to continue being affectionate until either I leave or she leaves. However, it never becomes easy. I've tried to take the same medicine I prescribe to others—giving hugs once a day whether I feel like it or not.

As bleak as the picture of people's shattered relationships may be, a wonderful ray of hope exists if we look at the original design for human beings expressed in Genesis. The six days of creation astound the mind, but the creation of men and women stands out as a particular masterpiece. As if God, in all His majesty, rolled up His sleeves, took His stance, and carefully, meticulously fashioned mankind in His own marvelous image. In order to progress toward identification of the broken pieces, now let us consider more closely what God originally fashioned.

For centuries there has been much discussion among biblical scholars about what it means to be made in God's image (Genesis

1:27). Many view it to mean we are like God in either form or function or both. While I suspect there may be some resemblance between God and human beings with regard to form, I strongly believe that the reference in the text deals more with function. In other words, being made in the image of God has little to do with form and everything to do with substance.

Regarding substance, being made in the image of God means that God, while having many unique attributes in His divine persona, reproduced a few of them in the men and women He created. Some of these transferred attributes would be sight (not necessarily physical sight, for the eyes are the window of the soul), reason, will, motion, breath, concern, hearing, smelling, tasting, and the capacity to love. There are other attributes that He reserves strictly for Himself. For example, omniscience, sovereignty, omnipotence, immutability, eternity, and infinity all belong to God alone. The attributes that God has transferred to us are the means by which we are to have dominion over all the earth.

Because of the entrance of sin into the human race through Adam, the original intention of God for human relationships became lost. Hence, we are a race of people whose relationships have sustained damage from hatred, greed, and selfishness. The Father's initial design was to use the union of marriage to demonstrate His love toward us. Society has decided instead to advocate the disposal of a partner who no longer pleases. Society is teaching to us to act as if there is an individual alive today with the ability to fully please us at all times.

A couple excited about their relationship came to me for premarital counseling. A wedding date had been set and invitations sent out. About three weeks before the wedding, the bride came to my office and shared her most recent discovery. Her fiancé was still seeing other women. I invited the man to my office and asked him to explain his behavior. He said, "Doc, this lady doesn't please me anymore. I'm not sure why she is upset. Just because I have something on lay-away doesn't mean I can't shop around." His statement proved his lack of understanding of God's plan. Of course, our discussion moved then to the ideas of honesty and commitment.

Where God created the family to be a unified group fostering and supporting one another, we now have family members in conflict with one another. When husband-and-wife relationships break down, of course, sibling relationships will follow. The husband and wife are models of what should go on in the home and set a good (or bad) example for their children. In most cases, adults testify that their parents didn't model a biblical relationship to them when they were young. Theirs were dysfunctional families, perverting the very purpose of God's intimacy—parents abusing children, children dishonoring their parents, and the like. Like the crack in the earth's core that continues to erode, the devastation of the family has led to the destruction of institutions and the respect once held for them. Neighbors who abuse their neighbors, police who violate their victims' civil rights, and, yes, politicians who abuse their constituents' trust, rights, and resources. There is no newspaper in America that does not validate these claims.

All this because of a few problems in relationships? Yes, indeed, for relationships are the very fabric of our society. In fact, there is no society, regardless of culture or race, that does not rest on this premise. The biblical account of God's love for mankind unfolds through the love, joy, and pain of the relationships Adam had with Eve, Cain had with Abel, Moses with Pharaoh, Joseph with his brothers, David with Jonathan, Jesus with His disciples, and Paul with Barnabas.

So is there any hope for us? The psalmist continually encourages us to have hope. For Christians and those who will allow the foundation of God to have its healing effect in their lives, there is certainly hope. I have discovered in my years of counseling that it is still God's design to mend relationships. Relationships are the means by which we begin the healing process.

Three

Shattered Relationships: As Old as the Fall

I want to make it clear that there are no perfect relationships. All of us struggle to some degree with the process of interaction with others. It would be wonderful if everything that I wanted to communicate was actually understood. Every relationship that I know of has some type of struggle, regardless of how much we pretend otherwise. Some do a better job of pretending than others. The fact remains that it is difficult for two people to come together and not have problems.

I asked a Catholic nun some time ago if she was really happy with her decision to remain single, and her reply was that she was happier than most married people. She said further that she feels sorry for many married people because they live in daily misery. If the truth were told, she is right. Many couples are enduring rather than enjoying their relationship. Think of the time that could be saved for fun activities if the times spent in disagreements were nil. However, our sin nature will not allow that to happen.

Romans 5:12 testifies that through one man (Adam) sin entered the world, and through sin, death came upon the human race. We often fail to appreciate the cunning and ferocity of the dynamic duo, sin and death. Sin is a brutal, pathological killer. For most people, it is actually a slow and torturous murderer, more deadly than the great white shark that prowls the seas looking for prey.

Every once in a while, we catch a headline that reminds us of this scourge of human existence. In 1994 a woman drove her car into a lake with her two infant children buckled in the rear seat. Before the car sank, she jumped out and left her two children to drown. She later told police that her children had been kidnapped and even went on national television pleading for her children's return. How could a person with such a disturbed mind not have troublesome relationships?

When we look at a tragedy like this, we are astonished, and we wonder about the crazy world we live in. We feel shock, anger, and sorrow. Yet somehow, knowing the testimony of Scripture with regard to man's evil insensitivity, one might wonder why chaotic events of this nature do not happen more often.

Suffice it to say, it is easy to look at the perpetrator of such a heinous crime and say, "She is a nut." That may well be true, but what causes one's behavior to derail to such an extent? Do not be surprised, for the possibility of such insanity resides in every man and woman. Given enough pressure, the tendency to slip out of control and act irrationally resides in all of us. Is it any wonder then that people in a loving relationship will deceive, lie, cheat, manipulate each other, and thereby create pain for each other? I encourage couples in my practice to be cautious as they depend on, believe in, and entrust their whole lives to each other. This may sound negative, but the fact is that no individual has the ability to meet all our needs and expectations.

Couples sometimes come to me expressing great shock that their mate could do this or that. They allow the shock of the behavior, not the behavior itself, to throw them into depression. My concern now shifts from their depression to the cause of it. Of course, when I observe that I am helping one who has completely trusted a human being and does not understand the Fall, I explain how foolish it is to trust people more than God, because any human being has the tendency to sin.

The thing that disturbs me most in my practice is the extent of denial that anything is wrong, especially coming from men. There are many theories about why men deny having problems. We know that the first step in getting well is admitting the need. Since resolving the problem may include dealing with emotions, many men don't even enter the process because they have been taught that expressing emotions is unmanly. For example, crying is not acceptable for a man in today's society.

Another reason it's difficult for men to admit to and deal with their problems is that many think their problem is a reflection of who they are. They have defined themselves and their self-worth by a negative behavior. If we were to allow our behavior to define us, none of us would be worth very much. Why? Because *all* of us are sinners, as Romans 3:23 points out. Each time I give a lecture, I ask my audience to define *all*. Though a rule of language forbids using a word to define itself, the last time I checked, *all* means all. Every one of us has been born with a sin nature—that is, a natural inclination to live our lives independent of God. We want to do our own thing. This tendency does not make most people homicidal maniacs. But it is a slow elixir of death in every human on this planet. My point is that our sin nature makes relationships very difficult.

Sin is calculating and meticulous in our lives. God warned Cain about the craftiness of sin, saying that sin "was crouching" at his door, longing to overtake him. Like a big cat on the hunt, sin toys with us. It grabs us and then sends us flying through the air. We are prisoners of its every whim.

Sin silently and subtly brings destruction to our lives. An example from nature shows how this principle of evil works. If a frog is placed in a kettle of boiling water, it will immediately try to jump out. However, if the frog is put in the water before it gets warm, and then the heat is gradually turned up, the frog will experience a slow and silent death.

The most remarkable thing about sin is that it can kill us by our own hand. Moreover, sin is not satisfied with our destruction only; it has great interest in watching us suffer as we perish. Sin enjoys inflicting pain through the relationships we try to keep. The question on the floor becomes whether or not it is possible for sinful people to have loving, fulfilling relationships.

God, in designing us after His image, fashioned us to be relaters—not just to relate, but to relate perfectly as He does. The Godhead, or the Trinity, provides an impeccable model of relating. God is a community of one, one in essence and being but three persons—the Father, the Son, and the Holy Spirit. They have existed together through eternity in perfect harmony. The harmony exists because of the holiness and love of God. All three persons of the Trinity agree, because they have the same righteous standard—to care for, cherish, and respect the others.

In order that man might properly bear the image of God, man had to exist in plurality like his Maker. God recognized this when He said, "It is not good for the man to be alone" (Genesis 2:18). It was not good because an environment of love was not possible until the advent of Eve into the Garden of Eden. Love by its very nature is oriented toward others. Love with just one person is an ego trip. God exists as a plural community of oneness, and thus His own handmade image-bearer who was to rule over the earth would also exist in a harmonious community characterized by love.

God took from the essence of man and made woman. As man and wife, Adam and Eve did a better job of bearing the image of God than just Adam alone. And as for love, Adam was so excited and eager to marry Eve, he performed the ceremony himself: "This is now bone of my bones and flesh of my flesh; she shall be called 'woman,' for she was taken out of man" (Genesis 2:23). God gave a hearty approval to this scenario: "God saw all that he had made, and it was very good" (Genesis 1:31). These new creatures were so good that God wanted Adam and Eve to continue to make other image-bearers: "Be fruitful and multiply."

Certainly love was an integral part of Adam and Eve's world, yet what held everything together was an atmosphere of holiness. This holiness was maintained through the relationship Adam and Eve had with God. Trust in God and obedience to God safeguarded Adam and Eve's relationship with one another. The holy instruction of God would not allow Adam to do anything that would bring pain into Eve's life, or vice versa. The success of their relationship depended totally upon their allegiance to God and His holy ways.

But this wonderful state of affairs came to an end at the tree of the knowledge of good and evil. After the first man and woman disobeyed God's explicit command, the positional holiness they held through their relationship with God dissipated. Sin is the absence of holiness. At the tree, sin crawled from its hiding place, bringing with it death—spiritual and eventually physical—and pain in relationships. The cancer in relationships would now reside in all future generations of dysfunctional image-bearers. Without God's holiness, the marriage made in Eden shattered.

Adam knew that the penalty for breaking fellowship with God was death. But he wanted to make it clear to God that the Fall was not his fault; rather it was "that woman's" fault, and it was God's fault for giving her to him. By pointing the finger at Eve, Adam was saying that Eve deserved the death penalty and not himself. What happened to that guy who was so eager to marry this girl that he performed his own ceremony? Now he was ready to see her die. If this wasn't a marriage on the rocks, I've never seen one that was.

The decline and fall of human relationships accelerated and proliferated. Every type of relationship felt the pinch and sting of sin as brother killed brother, friend killed friend, son lied to father, mother deceived father, daughters slept with fathers, and so on and so on. This pattern of shattered relationships continued all the way to Calvary. The fallenness of humanity was so profound that men killed the very Person who sought to save them from their sorrow.

The world teems with passionate and affectionate people; however, passion and affection do not necessarily mean love. Faulty facsimiles of love are dangerous. Anyone who enters a relationship without trusting and obeying God's instructions on how to love is essentially tap-dancing in a mine field. The dancing may be fun for a while, but sooner or later, an explosion will occur, and it won't be pretty. Yet many people are dead set on testing these turbulent waters, especially Christians who deceive themselves into believing that they have a relationship with God, when all they actually have is a ritual of attending church and saying amen to truths they never intend to apply.

Needless to say, because we are all born sinners, we enter the world as both potential agents and victims of sin. We are agents and victims in the context of relationships. God has designed us after His own image to be relaters, but because of our fallenness, we are incapable of properly bearing the image of God. Rather than being the standard, a caring and nurturing relationship is by far the exception. When we do "what comes naturally," our relationships tend to be debilitating. Sinfulness in relationships causes pain, which in turn cracks and shatters our worlds, our lives, our hopes, and our loves.

Sin confuses the senses. When a person is under its control, it's as if he is lost in a forest without a compass. Each step he takes, he becomes more lost than he was before. To make matters worse, he seems to hear voices all around calling, "This is the way out." The truth is that there is no way out. The only way is up!

By contrast, in the relationship of God the Father, God the Son, and God the Holy Spirit, we have an example of perfection—no jealousy, envy, strife, selfishness, and so on. It seems to me that in order for the people of God to have healthy relationships, we must constantly submit ourselves to God. Only in this way can we rid ourselves of selfishness, insecurity, greed, hate, lack of self-control, immorality, and all that destroys our relationships with one another.

Four

A Closer Look

When someone's world shatters, that person needs to take a step backward and reflect on the dynamics in his or her family of origin. A person's early interaction with parents, siblings, or other relatives may shape present perceptions and problems. Feelings of failure, depression, hopelessness, or helplessness often arise from these childhood relationships.

From all my work with hurting people, I know well that past emotional wounds can cause present pain. Unaddressed pain distorts our ability to relate to God and or to other people. Ultimately, the distortion inhibits our ability to experience an abundant life in Christ.

Everyone has suffered some degree of relational pain during development. It would be great to receive all the nurturing necessary to develop without emotional deficits; however, no one has a perfect upbringing. Some receive too much attention from parents or teachers, while others do not receive enough. Some are forced into roles of responsibility before they are developmentally prepared, and others are stifled and prevented from assuming responsibility. Some have experienced abandonment, and some have been overly sheltered.

We all have experienced imperfect relationships, and the result is relational baggage.

The home environment is where we should receive the motivation and modeling for emotional growth. For many people, however, that environment contained much that hindered healthy development. The result is a self-image wrapped in a cocoon of messages that are contrary to what God says about us. Though new creatures in Christ, many believers must now work through that hardened shell of distortion before they can experience new life as Christ intends.

When an event in life occurs, we filter it through a grid of personal experience, knowledge, and perception in order to determine how we will think or act in response. The manner in which we perceive the world, others, and ourselves determines our outlook on life. Therefore, whenever we experience emotions such as depression, self-doubt, and other negative feelings in relationships, we must probe the thoughts and analyze the attitudes behind our feelings. After identifying the erroneous belief, we must work to reconstruct our mental processes. The degree to which we place our thoughts under the lordship of Christ will determine how much we attain in our walk with Him.

There's No Place Like Home

A well-known poem is entitled, "Children Learn What They Live." It lists the lessons learned by both positive and negative home environments. The poem communicates a message: Who we are today is a direct result of how we were raised. It is true that interaction in the family of origin is very much woven into the fabric of our belief system. Principles transferred to us during our rearing provide the foundation upon which we base our actions. It is in the home that our introduction to relationships occurs.

Some psychologists argue that this introduction actually begins in the womb. One of my patients held this point of view, and she came to me concerned about the child she carried in her womb. During her first pregnancy, she and her husband had divorced. At that time she experienced great emotional turmoil and did not have positive feelings about her pregnancy. As she sat across from me during a session, she expressed her concern for her oldest son. Her belief, a conclusion based upon her son's behavior, was that he experienced low self-esteem and felt unwanted no matter how much she told him otherwise. She believed that his feelings stemmed from her emotional instability prior to his birth. Then the client said to me, "During my pregnancy, I was so upset, constantly fighting with my husband, that I wished I wasn't pregnant. I wanted to die, and all those negative feelings affected my son." Now that she was pregnant again and going through a second divorce, she wanted to expedite the reconciliation between herself and her estranged husband so that negative in-utero effects would not occur with her second child.

Whether or not her unborn child would be adversely affected cannot be concretely determined. It is clear, however, that what we experience from our parents before the age of six has immense impact on who we are today. Interaction with family members, whether positive or negative, has a profound effect on how we develop. The book of Proverbs is full of wise instructions to parents to exercise discipline when violations occur at an early stage of a child's life. If we wait until they are teenagers, we've waited too long.

The home has an influence on its members that no other institution has. In our families of origin, we receive motivation and modeling for life. As a child interacts with others in the household, he or she adopts mannerisms and forms inclinations and personal preferences. No two households are identical. Children who are reared in houses next door to each other develop differently. The children of one family may enjoy Asian food and love to travel, while the children of the other family may favor Italian food and relish quiet evenings at home. The differences in development result primarily from parental influence on the lives of the children.

Some parents teach their children that life is wonderful. They provide positive reinforcement and emphasize the opportunities open to everyone. Their children adopt this outlook and grow up to act upon it.

Other parents teach their children that life is not fair or that it is a war zone, or that they are superior because of color or ability. These children also believe what they have been taught and in turn act on it. Parents play a vital role in determining the nature of the relationships—loving, sharing, trusting, supporting—in the home. Each child reared in that setting will be a unique tapestry of the influence and impact the parents had on his or her life.

Relationships in our family of origin also influence our emotional development. Each one of us has an innate need for love, security, attachment, and acceptance. As we grew, it was the role of our first family to provide the nurture, respect, discipline, protection, and support for positive development. No family is perfect, but each has the responsibility to be a context in which love, support, guidance, and discipline for the children are provided in a manner that builds character and self-esteem. When I look at my patients, it is evident that some families do provide the basic building blocks for positive development.

But parenting and building a positive family life take work, and sometimes parents fail to put forth that extra effort. When children do not see examples of positive interaction in the home, they grow up with emotional and relational deficits. In homes where family relations are more like a battlefield, a crisis mentality develops, and people suffer from feelings of guilt and shame.

There are various reasons why relationships in the home are not fashioned the way God intends. Many have found themselves in the role of parent without prior consideration of the task. Because they did not ask for the role, they may reject it by abandoning their responsibility. Others may respond in anger, abusing their authority and punishing rather than nurturing. Still others, in ignorance of God's instructions, do what is natural to them.

The result is children who do not know how to love, how to care, and how to contribute to society. They take refuge in the occult, drugs, sexuality, alcoholism, and gangs. That fewer families are building strong relationships is evident in the accelerated divorce rate, the increasing drug use, and the mounting gang violence occurring in communities today. Mom and Dad are more interested in politics, sex, money, building careers, etc., than in building their homes. Though those interests are not wrong in and of themselves, prioritizing them over one's children is.

In order to develop successful family relationships, there must be a Christ-centered foundation upon which to build all decisions, attitudes, and actions. Without this focus, there is no sure model to follow when people face the pressures that confront every family.

No one is born with an instruction manual. There are no prerequisites one must meet in order to be a parent, and one is not interviewed before becoming a member of a family. Only on-the-job training is available. But when Christ is the focus, His grace covers human error. In Christ we have the assurance that our families are a blessing from God, and we can approach the task of relating with confidence. Interaction with one another in the fear and admonition of the Lord yields hope that God will honor our efforts to bring glory to Him. This outlook on relationships provides encouragement that can be channeled into positive interaction with others.

Speed Trap

In a society where we are accustomed to "instant," "fast," and "micro," we must remind ourselves that there are no magical solutions to the challenges of relationships. In our endeavor to provide a firm foundation for emotional health, we must be willing to invest sufficient time. It may not be our intention to bulldoze the needs of family, friends, and other believers; however, in hot pursuit of our own happiness, that often happens.

The ideal American time line is the primary reason many rush through life. It dictates that one must be married and begin a family by thirty, have a stable career by thirty-five, educate one's children and be able to retire in style by sixty-five.

Too often single Christians subconsciously respond to the invisible pressure by rushing into marriage as soon as they meet a prospective mate. The major questions to ask when contemplating matrimony are overlooked because, after all, there may never be another chance like this one. Underlying fear prevents the cultivation of a healthy relationship.

When I think of a healthy relationship, I envision one in which both partners experience the proper stages for growth—the romantic, the reality, and the responsibility stages.

In the romantic stage of a relationship, the couple is "in love" and even "in like." This is the phase I call the drug-induced stage. "I have found Mr. Right or Miss Right." "He is so wonderful." "She is a fox—long legs, fat lips, etc." "I even like how he chews his food." The major things are overlooked, and both partners are lost in the euphoria of being in each other's presence. Focus is more on feelings and on physical appearance. There is no problem with the negative aspects of the other person. The negative in most cases is not even seen because so much attention is paid to the physical. If one party says he or she has just come out of drug rehabilitation or has been bisexual, such statements do not even register. The other party will say, "No problem, everyone makes mistakes," "I'll change him," or "We can pray through this one." Something other than reality is driving the relationship.

Most likely, the perception each has of the other is the image each person has tried to project. Though there may be some great fun when the two are together, each is relating with a chameleon. Invisible walls are up so that neither partner can see the other's true colors. Many marriages of couples in this stage begin in the drive-through chapels of Las Vegas and end up in divorce courts because of "incompatibility." And I want to raise a caution for those interacting on this level of relationship. Sexual compromise has caused many single Christians to marry before they should or to break off relationships that could have blossomed.

I believe that the pressure of the culture pushes couples to get serious quickly. However, that does not have to be the case. In other cultures, one can enter into friendships without marriage in mind. It is from friendship that the more serious relationship develops.

The reality stage hits after the couple has been dating awhile and gets to know each other more intimately. When reality kicks in, the relationship may cool off for a while. Often the two break up and move on to new partners because of unwillingness to deal with the difficult issues that are now part of the dynamics. If the couple decides they still want to pursue a deeper relationship, then they make the total commitment of marriage and accept the responsibility of that commitment.

I also see the effect of the "speed trap" in the average household. Because parents are trying to do the best they can, time with the children is often sacrificed. Some parents devote their energy to the tasks of the work day and have none to invest in their household when they return home. Leaving early in the morning to perform a good day's work and returning home late in the evening "to rest" for the next day becomes the daily grind.

Confused priorities foster the idea that all of one's energy should be used at the office and that home is for rest. I am amazed by the number of husbands who tell me, "She won't let me rest when I come home. I just want to sit on the sofa and watch television." That type of existence may have worked for Ozzie and Harriet or the Cleavers, but Father definitely does not know best if that is his attitude.

Lasting relationships require a new mentality about home. Each day, instead of thinking we are going home to rest, we should know we are going home to work. In the home our work is not toilsome, but it is a labor of love. Spiritual, emotional, and physical needs of the family must be addressed on a daily basis. These tasks are just as important as what is done in the workplace. Each one's part is necessary for enrichment of the other family members. Children need interaction with the parents, parents need interaction with the children, and spouses need interaction with one another.

Observation of distressed families reveals how many Christians have succumbed to the idea that providing money or material things equals love. Consequently, parents sacrifice the time that should be spent creating joyful memories with the family in order to work to buy their happiness. A young man named Bernie came to my office after he had experienced the devastating effects of cocaine addiction. He was the son of a wealthy family. When he was a small boy, he had longed for his father's attention. Instead of time, the father gave him money and instructed his son to play with his friends. As Bernie grew older, he and his friends began to spend the money his father supplied on cocaine.

During one of my counseling sessions, I asked Bernie what he regretted most about his life. He told me that his greatest sorrow was that his father did not want to spend time with him. In a subsequent session at which Bernie and his father were both present, he implored his father to look at him. "See what your money has done; I am a cocaine addict. All I wanted was you—not your money." The tears that flowed from their eyes expressed the remorse and regret that failure to invest in relationships causes.

Imperfect Parents

The Bible instructs us to "train up a child in the way he should go, and when he is old, he will not depart from it." This passage did not say to let children raise themselves up in the way they should go, but we live in a generation where children are raising themselves. The word *train* implies work, not rest. Often we read this verse and focus our attention on child discipline. However, it takes more than just disciplining a child to train him "in the way he should go." In order to do what God has commanded us to do, we must spend time getting acquainted with the individual personalities of our children. We must talk to them, play with them, and encourage them to pursue goals that are in line with their individual strengths and abilities.

There are many benefits in training children this way. One of the most obvious is the confidence and value instilled in the child by this investment of time. The second is the intangible self-esteem planted into the heart of the child.

To build strong family relationships, nurturing attention is needed. Studies show that a living being who does not receive physical and emotional love will withdraw and ultimately die. So many children in our communities are not receiving the nurture they need to mature into healthy adults. Emotional neglect usually does not result in physical death, but it leaves scars on one's personality, with the habits of withdrawal, recurrent anger, hatred, or depression afflicting one's life and relationships.

Instead of giving the time and attention necessary to explain and direct childhood behavior, some parents rely on destructive techniques to maintain control. As we probe the negative methods used in parenting, you may see your own story. You may be on the receiving end of these practices, or you may be using these methods yourself in the relationships with your spouse, your children, or your friends. As you reflect on your own history, it is important that you forgive those who have hurt you. Some may have already forgiven; others may need to work toward accomplishing that task. If you are the perpetrator, ask God for His forgiveness and then forgive yourself—and begin making some changes.

Measuring by Performance

Popeye, the famous one-eyed cartoon character, used to say, "I am what I am and that's all that I am." If I were to restate his remark to characterize the effect of a bad parenting technique, the child might say, "I am what I do, and that's all that I am." Here the parent has identified the child by what he or she does, using behavior to define existence, until the child adopts this identity. When the child steals, he is labeled a thief. When the child does not tell the truth, she is branded a liar. A child who constantly hears that he or she is a liar or a thief will begin to believe it. Liar, thief comes to sum up the child's whole identity.

What we do does not determine who we are, but rather what we do is merely our behavior. There is a difference between who we are in Christ and what we do as sinful human beings. Romans 5:8 states that while we were yet sinners, still not performing well, Christ died for us. We have a responsibility to watch what we say to our children. Their stealing is wrong behavior, but that doesn't determine who they are. Almost everyone stole as a child; are we all thieves? There is a difference between who we are and what we do, and this difference must be clearly explained to our children when they misbehave. Wrong behavior must be corrected, but the identity of the child is not equivalent with the negative behavior.

I have had several clients who suffered greatly from being compared unfavorably with siblings or other children. These clients had developed overwhelming feelings of inadequacy. Often those who are held up as the "standard" are uncomfortable with the practice as well. In either case, favoritism relays the message that, whether one is condemned or praised, both individuals are defined by performance.

Disrespect

Another technique parents may use to gain control is disrespect. Though children are small, they need to be heard. Children may be loud, hyperactive, and impulsive, but they are full of ideas and thoughts. Their job is to play. It is through play that they experience the world around them. When parents hurry their children to grow up so that the parents do not have to suffer the "inconvenience" of dealing with childishness too long, they are ignoring the need for the children to grow, explore, and inquire at their own pace. When parents do not accept normal childhood behavior and attempt to quell a child's enthusiasm for life, the child rebels.

Children cry out for respect. Even though they are small, they are human beings too. They need to be accepted, heard, and taught. When we respect them, they grow to respect others. In the violence perpetrated by children, we see young people who have been pushed to the periphery of life. Although they may not have been aborted, children who are treated as major inconveniences have been denied time and the intimacy of family life. At an early age, parents rush children to day care or schools to be taught by people with whom they have no personal relationships.

The resulting confusion about who they are impairs children's ability to properly relate to others. They exhibit extreme behavior, ranging from selfishness to a tendency to be overly self-sacrificing. The demand for respect through violence or the self-effacing behavior of compromise typifies those who did not receive respect during their development.

Perhaps you were a child whose parents or other caregivers did not know how to keep in balance the need to discipline and the need to show respect. In their discipline, they may have intermingled reproof and ridicule. The motivation of making you, as a child, "feel bad" about doing something wrong may have delivered a fatal blow to your self-worth. If your inability to contribute positively to relationships results from lack of respect during your development, there is hope for you in Christ. He has made it possible for you to approach God Himself and make your concerns known. God is omniscient. He knows your story, and He cares about you.

Let me encourage you not to feel ashamed of your struggle. Some Christians feel that all aspects of life must be going perfectly simply because they know the Lord. Many churches and Christian groups teach such ideas. May I suggest that knowing the Lord doesn't mean that you won't have struggles. There are many examples of people who knew the Lord and yet went through many trials in life. Don't deny your struggles. Make them a matter of prayer daily and find a godly brother or sister or counselor with whom you can share them and receive counsel. You are not the only one with problems.

Negative Prophecies

"You will never amount to anything." "You will always be trouble." "You can't do anything right." Many children grow up hearing these kinds of predictions about their future, and the destructive forecasts stored in their memory banks haunt their existence. As adults, these people define themselves in terms of these negative opinions. Condemning prophecies stunt the growth of people whom God intended to be free and to "reign" in life. The pain of feeling worthless and hopeless paralyzes people, leaving them empty and unable to attain the position in life God designed for them.

Often those who attempt in their own strength to prove the prophecies untrue end up damaging their emotional and physical health. The pressure of living to invalidate the prophecies of others has serious consequences. Often ulcers, heart attacks, strokes, and other physical ailments result from the self-imposed perfectionistic attempts to prove one's parents wrong.

It is important for us to realize that the perceptions others have of us do not determine who we are. God has a plan for each of us, and only He determines what we can become. I encourage people to be careful about putting all their eggs in a human basket. Human beings change their minds all the time because of their sin nature.

I had a client who accepted every analysis of others about her. To make my point, I called her ugly, and she expressed shock that her counselor would also have a negative opinion of her. Then I told her that if she gives me one thousand dollars, my opinion will change. She will then become the most beautiful person on earth. My point was that human beings change their minds all the time based on circumstances, but our mighty God does not. So if God has said that she is beautiful and wonderfully made, why should she listen to me?

Disallowing Choices

Perhaps one of the most detrimental parenting techniques is disallowing choices. The harmful effects of this practice dominate the lives of many Christians. Adults who have trusted Christ are paralyzed in their ability to take the "risks" necessary to do what God wants done. Following God takes faith. Doing what the Holy Spirit guides us to do requires us to believe in what we cannot see.

Submitting to God's authority and living according to His plan is a decision, a choice, that each of us has to make. We achieve the abundant spiritual life He promises when we apply His commands and instructions to our lives. Some of the pain and trouble we experience today is caused by our fear of doing what God wants us to do. We seek God's direction and His power, but we don't follow through at the point of implementation. Fear of the unknown overtakes us, and we seek others' opinions and approval instead of doing what the Spirit of God has directed us to do. The resulting guilt and feelings of failure cause much pain.

For many the inability to depend upon God, make a decision, and follow through with it stems from a failure to learn these skills during our childhood. If our parents did not create scenarios conducive to the development of our ability to make decisions, we are handicapped in this area. We must seek opportunities now as adults to develop this skill.

It is important to give small children the opportunity to choose things, such as the cereal they eat for breakfast, their preference of milk or orange juice, or the cartoon they want to watch. Given two or three choices and the freedom to choose, children soon develop confidence in their ability to make decisions. As the child grows, freedom of choice can be extended to many other areas—for example, to the color of dress. Teenagers should be given an opportunity to choose their friends and extracurricular activities. All of their choices, however, must be within God's guidelines.

Just as we have liberty in the Holy Spirit within the boundary of God's commandments, children should be given freedom within boundaries. When parents do not allow children to make choices, the inevitable problems result. As children grow, they will depend upon others to make decisions for them. Friends, the "crowd," what "everybody else" is doing replace the parent as the decision-maker. In marriages, one person may be overly reliant upon the spouse to make decisions. In other instances, an adult child may still call Mom or Dad for an opinion on whom to date, what decision to make, or to settle an argument.

Scripture is clear on God's desire for us to develop the ability to trust Him, make a decision, and follow through. Jesus was not a mama's boy. In the account of the wedding feast at Cana, Mary sought to use her position as mother to influence His actions. Though He did not disrespect her, He made it clear that His actions would be based on God's timing in His life and not on hers. Her response was to allow Him that choice—an example of how parents must surrender control to God in the lives of their children.

Since surrender of authority will eventually occur in all parent-child relationships, parents must help their children develop powerful tools to overcome the obstacles to a fruitful life. Adults who did not learn this skill as children will have to begin working at developing it now. However, it is important to know that after one has made the decision to trust Christ as personal Savior, He provides the assurance that all choices in line with His will are best and that all power necessary to succeed in those choices is guaranteed.

Social Expectations

Three years after I became a Christian, God placed a desire within me to pursue full-time ministry. Now it must be understood that in my Nigerian culture, there are definite expectations for the firstborn child. As the eldest son, I was expected to be successful, take care of my parents, and have a "real job." When I told my parents of God's call into the ministry, they were astonished. For three years, my father did not want to speak to me and would not allow positive interaction because I was outside of his will. He considered it a disgrace that his eldest son would choose to become "little more than a beggar."

Relatives who sympathized with my father expressed their condolences to my mother for the loss of her eldest son. Since I was expected to go away and become a great surgeon, a renowned engineer, or a distinguished scientist, my choice of "a poor minister's life" was cause for grief. Concerned neighbors would look at me pitifully and apologize to my mom and dad for the loss of their son.

Whether it is the American dream of a lovely home, two cars, and 2.5 over-achieving children, or the village expectations for the eldest child to become a great success and provide financial stability for aging parents, all societies have expectations for those who live within them. Though it is desirable to have goals and standards, when we fail to realize those expectations, we feel pain. There are financial expectations, educational expectations, cultural expectations, career expectations, and familial expectations. The pressures to comply may be applied by peers, parents, or the media. Regardless of the source, each of us to some degree has been affected by the expectations to maintain the status quo and approach the milestones of life at the accepted pace. Since societal standards are inculcated into our own lives, we evaluate our successes and failures based upon how well we meet them.

Psychology suggests that each individual should take an inventory of his or her life. The pivotal time for this assessment is usually between the ages of thirty-five and forty. When people look back at their lives to assess progress, they must see that their own expectations in each of these areas have been realized. If, in their opinion, they have not attained their goals, they feel a sense of failure and sadness. If the sadness is prolonged, it will become hopelessness. This hopelessness, if allowed to persist, transforms into helplessness. With the passage of time, helplessness becomes a sense of worthlessness. Finally the lingering feeling of worthlessness develops into depression. The feelings of failure, hopelessness, worthlessness, and depression can be so strong they drive the person to suicide.

A woman scheduled an appointment with me on her thirty-fifth birthday. During our session, I asked her why she decided to see me on that particular day. She explained that she did not feel like celebrating her birthday because she had accomplished nothing with her life. She said that she had expected to be married by the time she was thirty years old and to be purchasing her home. She expected to have children, but she wanted a father for those children in the home. In her plan for herself, she had envisioned a successful career in which she would be handsomely compensated; however, none of these things were realized. In her assessment, she was a failure because what she had planned for herself did not materialize by the time she was thirty-five. Her self-concept was totally dependent on fulfilling these hopes.

It is extremely dangerous to give societal expectations the place of final authority in your life. Because societal standards are not based upon objective standards, they are subject to change and frequently do. When the situations in life change, the opinions of people change as well. During the 1960s, the familial standard for women changed from working primarily in the home to a career outside the home. In America the societal craze is a perfect body; so people are devoting an enormous amount of time in the gym and health clubs exercising until they are too sore to move the next morning. In other cultures, however, to be thin indicates poverty; therefore, the societal standard encourages one to be well-fed, and to be overweight is not considered a problem.

Though we may use the societal standards that do not conflict with the Word of God as guideposts, we must understand that even then God has complete sovereignty. Because societal expectations change and cannot be trusted as a final basis for assessing our lives, we must seek a higher authority. We must realize that God is the Master Planner and that He has our lives from our birth until our death in His control. He does not define us based on what our society says we should do. He tells us to delight ourselves in Him, and He will give us the desires of our heart.

However, His blessings are not regulated by the timetable of any society. He may plan for one person to experience certain benefits at age twenty-five and for another to experience those same blessings at sixty. Why listen to fickle human beings who change their minds, as opposed to Christ who never changes His mind? We can depend on Him because He is the same yesterday, today, and forever. Christ gives us the correct standard against which we are to evaluate our lives, so the pain and pressure of societal expectations do not have to be the ultimate authority for the man or woman who follows the Lord.

Part Two

The Puzzle Without Peace

Five

Pain That Impedes Progress

It is not enough to look in retrospect to see where we have come from; the journey toward reparation of a broken world must also include an assessment of where we stand today. Personal hang-ups, to use a modern colloquialism, place an almost unbearable weight on the shoulders of believers. Struggling to keep an emotional and spiritual balance becomes a true juggling act. The weight of misperceptions begins to overload the believer as they are carried day after day, until finally the Christian breaks. The person who seemed to have it all together now faces the emotional, physical, and spiritual devastation of a life that has fallen apart. One wonders what in the world went wrong.

Remember, Jesus said, "Take my yoke upon you and learn of me, for I am gentle and humble in heart, and you will find rest for your souls. For *my yoke* is easy and *my burden* is light." When I look into the faces of many Christians, I see the discouragement and frustration that comes from carrying a heavy load. Year after year people struggle under the weight until they reach a breaking point. Because Christ's yoke is easy, I know that the load borne is not one He has placed there. The burden is most often picked up as a result of attitudes derived from fiction rather than from the facts of Scripture.

Each day the believer must ask, "What actions and attitudes presently inhibit a fruitful Christian life for me? Are there practices and perspectives that prevent the Holy Spirit from possessing all of me?" Let's look at some of the common factors in our inability to be healthy partners in relationships and to experience all that God would have us enjoy in our walk with Him.

Fear of Relationship

The clarity of God's call to dynamic interrelation with others is undeniable. In both the written Word of God and in the nature of human beings, God has made the need for interaction apparent. The Bible tells us that before God formed Eve, the Trinity contemplated Adam's environment. Land, sea, and animals had been created, and God said they were good. When God looked at His finished creation of Adam, He also said His work was good. However, when the Godhead considered Adam in relation to the world in which he was to live, God said that it was *not good* for Adam to be alone. Even in a perfect world, God believed man needed companionship and lifelong relationship. In meeting this need, God established marriage. And of the unity between man and wife Scripture says, "For this reason a man will leave his father and mother and be united to his wife, and they will become one flesh" (Genesis 2:24).

Our human nature manifests the need for relationships throughout our daily routines. We organize, socialize, fellowship, and marry to associate with others. It is normal and healthy to need others.

A plethora of examples of relationships exists throughout the Word of God. Scripture supports the idea that human beings are created with a need for others. In the book of Proverbs, we are told: "As iron sharpens iron, so one man sharpens another" (Proverbs 27:17). Relationships among believers are encouraged in Hebrews 10 where the writer tells this small church not to abandon the assembly of believers. In the context of dynamic interaction, God intends for us to develop physically, emotionally, and spiritually. From creation until today, He has said that it is not good for man or woman to be alone. In that first instance, He created Eve, a helper for Adam. Today, through relationships, God seeks to satisfy our innate longing for affiliation and affirmation.

It is God's intent for each of us to have healthy relationships within our families and our churches. But for many Christians, the area of relationships causes great fear. We fear failure, and we fear rejection. Each of us has experienced the fear of failure. In a society that focuses heavily on success, the fear of failure keeps many from even trying to form close relationships. Thus, they avoid the pain and discouragement that could result.

And all of us have experienced the paralysis the fear of rejection causes. Even when we know how to handle another's disapproval, we are susceptible to this fear. We are prone to it because of the message it communicates—we did not measure up to someone else's standards. Our fears may be founded on actual experiences, or they may be only our perception of what other people think of us. It would be good if our fear promoted emotional health, but it does not. Whether fear of rejection or failure, fear restricts our ability to interact as God intends. Scripture informs us that God has not given us a spirit of fear, but one of power and a sound mind. So if our withdrawal from interaction is based on the fear of rejection, we are not acting in harmony with the Holy Spirit who dwells within us. Our behavior runs counter to His nature. In doing so, we grieve Him. When we grieve the Spirit of God, we suffer.

At times the fear of relationship results in a tendency to rely on the experiences of others instead of risking the unknown in one's own interaction with someone. People seek advice from friends, coworkers, call-in talk show hosts, or acquaintances at the neighborhood bar for problems in personal relationships. Those looking for answers feel more comfortable depending on what others say happened to them in a similar situation, even though the results of someone else's experience are not necessarily appropriate in these cases. Many find it more comfortable to end their troubled relationships than to encounter unfamiliar terrain. Some find themselves choosing paths that have been tried by others even though those paths lead to places (or patterns of interaction) where they do not wish to go.

Sue knew that the relationship between her mom and dad was dysfunctional. As a young woman, she decided she would never enter into a relationship that would become as painful as the one she witnessed between her parents. She decided to go to college and pursue a career in hope that she would be different and that her life would not be lived with regrets. Although the reasons for her parents' tumultuous marriage were unknown to Sue, the result of her observations was a subconscious decision never to marry. She had concluded that since marriage is so painful, the way to avoid pain is to stay single. Her mother contributed to this attitude toward matrimony by steering Sue in the direction of pursuing higher education and of seeking fulfillment in activities other than marriage and family. After all, if Sue could take care of herself, there would be no need for dependence on someone else.

But something began to happen to upset Sue's plans. She began to hear the tick of her "biological clock" and longed for marriage and children. When she did marry, however, the cycle of dysfunction continued. She married because she did not want to be alone, but even in marriage she wanted to remain autonomous for fear of dependency. After all, she had devoted the major portion of her college and career to establishing herself so that she would never need a man. But her independence caused problems in her marriage.

The fear of relational dependency often causes couples to lead separate lives in the same house—mere coexistence. Cohabitation can be described as a relationship in which interaction occurs on an "as-needed" basis. In some contexts this kind of relationship is appropriate. Members of an athletic team must work together to defeat an opponent, but they do not have to enjoy deep, personal interaction with one another. In the workplace, it is common for personality clashes to prevent the development of relationships, but because workers have specified objectives, each overlooks his personal preferences and contributes to the attainment of the company goal.

I used to wonder what happens in the cheerleader squad when members don't get along—particularly when they build formations such as a human pyramid. My thinking was that a girl who did not like another squad member might let her slip through her hands. But then a client of mine who was a cheerleader and who was having problems with another cheerleader said to me, "I may hate her, but when we get together to practice, I'm able to let go of my feelings to get the job at hand done."

In school and in the workplace, it may be acceptable and comfortable for relationships to remain superficial. The individuals interacting in those environments have their own personal worlds in which they relate. However, when the superficial mode of interaction invades the personal relationships of home and church, a substantial amount of pain results.

This type of association continues on a solely functional basis. In the home the husband and wife live together for economic reasons or as a sexual arrangement or for the sake of the children. There is little genuine interest in the relationship or emotional intimacy. Both parties may be amicable, and both take care of the important functions of the household, but the relationship is devoid of dynamic interpersonal interest and love. Marriages characterized by coexistence are often held together by legalism. If the couple did not believe that it is a "sin to get a divorce" (apart from sexual immorality), they would race to the county courthouse, or one might seriously pray that the other will have an affair in order to provide a biblical reason for the faithful spouse to leave. Or perhaps social pressure—through family, friends, or employment—keeps the couple together.

It is important to note that when married couples merely coexist, the impact of dysfunction extends beyond the husband and wife. Not only are *they* miserable, but the children reared in the home will be subject to emotional dysfunction as well. Children observe the method of relationship exemplified by their parents. They accept it as the right way to relate, and a home where the parents do not have a sincere interest in each other produces children who will not know how to show interest in others either.

I remember as a boy noticing the peculiar behavior chickens exhibited when they were placed in new surroundings. When the chicken was placed on the ground, she would stand on one leg—keeping the other leg bent closely against her body. Gradually, as the chicken became comfortable with her surroundings, she would lower the bent leg, retracting it at the slightest threat. Only when the chicken was confident that the environment presented no danger would she keep both legs on the ground and become calm.

For many Christians, relationships present new environments packed with uncertainty. As a result, they approach friendships, courtship, and marriage as did the chickens I observed as a child. Fear of the unknown causes them to retract emotional involvement although they may offer physical interaction with others. Fear of the unknown keeps them from fully participating in relationships.

The fear may result from messages a person received during the process of maturation. One may have been told not to trust members of the opposite sex because they were only out to get what they could in a relationship. Many a young woman is told to go to school and get a college degree because she could not depend on a man to provide for her. Men who fear emotional intimacy have been told not to become vulnerable because a woman's only intentions are to manipulate. Others may be afraid of fully participating in relationships because they have been hurt before. Past relational anguish sometimes hurts so much that, though the wounded person may be willing to function in other relationships, any real emotional sharing presents too high a risk. Those who have been wounded settle for coexistence instead of risking repeated pain.

Stepparents are highly susceptible to slipping into coexistence with a mate. Because the parent of the children needs to work through the pain of the breakup of the last relationship, he or she may have difficulty trusting the new spouse. As a consequence, they fail to develop an emotional union.

It is important, for this reason, for single parents considering marriage to be sure they have worked through their past pain and are willing to allow the prospective mate to become an emotional, supportive parent to the children. These single parents must be careful not to let their children's anger and resentment at the loss of the biological parent hinder the couple's own emotional bonding with each other.

I encourage potential couples to go through premarital counseling to make sure they will afford their spouse-to-be full opportunity to be involved in the lives of the children from previous relationships. Another reason I encourage premarital counseling is to cultivate interaction between the children and the spouse-to-be before the wedding. Several men that I counsel feel resentment toward the spouse and the stepchildren when they are not allowed to be fully involved in parenting those children. They feel used, thinking, *All I am good for is providing food and shelter.*

Churches also present opportunities for coexistence. Many who volunteer countless hours of their time merely coexist with other Christians. The same fear that paralyzes family relationships also grips the interaction between brothers and sisters in Christ. Meetings are held, programs are planned, financial goals are attained, and ministry to the unsaved is performed without the close association of the members who give of themselves. Pain experienced from criticism or past situations prevents believers from participating emotionally in Christian fellowship.

Satan uses the tool of coexistence effectively to keep us from experiencing the joy God intends for us. The lack of trust arising from past pain must be worked through in order to move forward in our Christian walk.

A Need to Please

Each of us is a unique masterpiece created by the Master Artist. With meticulous detail, God has crafted our physical and emotional components to make each person unique. There are no duplicates. As we relate to one another, it is important for us to understand that no two people are identical. Each of us approaches life from the vantage point that exists behind our eyes in our own brain or psyche.

In a world that seeks to make everyone the same, it is likely we will seize on errant ways of relating in an effort to prevent rejection. This maladjustment results from our attempts to manage the fear of existing without being loved. We may not have developed a strong sense of identity, so we tend to become overinvolved in everyone else's life. This failure to know who we are comes in part from neglecting the development of personal likes, dislikes, and interests.

Those who never came to a sense of identity or who have lost it are afraid of being alone or abandoned. Their behavior is marked by a desire to lean on someone stronger and by avoidance of stating opinions. Those who operate out of this fear have no clear direction for their lives and go along with others so they will not be rejected.

To avoid being abandoned, people may overlook the need to draw healthy relational boundaries, permitting others to interfere in their lives who have no right to do so. Often the interaction of parents, children, friends, and extended family may wreak havoc to the primary relationship. However, the fear of living alone and being abandoned results in a lack of proper boundaries. In enmeshed relationships, there is no separation between one's own interests and the interests of everyone else. In marital relationships, the husband or wife cannot give the foremost commitment to the spouse because the affairs of the children, parents, aunts, uncles, nieces, or nephews are brought into the primary relationship.

In my counseling, I have observed instances in which a parent feels unable to let go of an inappropriate relationship with a son or daughter in order to develop a relationship with the spouse because the parent expects the child to be their future social security. In marriages that involve a stepparent, I often find a spouse who cannot let go of a child because the child became a friend during the time of singleness. Now that a mate is present, the lack of boundaries in relating to the child prevents the marriage relationship from gelling.

In the husband-wife relationship, the most important person should always be the spouse. There is no family, friend, coworker, church member, or other person who should take priority over one's mate. However, when relationships are enmeshed, it is common for others to be drawn into the interaction, discussions, and decisions that should be managed between the couple. There has to be a proper boundary between the marriage relationship and the children, parents, family, and friends. At times this limit extends to what is said in the presence of the children and others. At other times, caution must be observed with regard to physical interaction and intimacy before the children in the household.

Even when we relate to others, we must remember that God created us as individuals and that there is a balance between relating to others and developing ourselves. Because one is married does not mean that one does not have a life of one's own. It is okay to be married and have individual interests as long as those interests enhance the common goals of the family. We must still pay attention to our individual needs and interests.

God has given the husband the role of setting the agenda for the family, and He has given the wife the role of supporting him as the family aspires to that goal. However, God did not diminish individual skills, abilities, and creativity when He assigned those roles. He expects us to operate within the guidelines while fully utilizing our individual strengths to attain those goals.

In any relationship, there is a need for both bonding and boundaries—between husband and wife, between parents and children, between the married couple and family, and between friends. The two concepts are not mutually contradictory. And there may be times when the word no is appropriate with people in relationships. I strongly believe that no is a complete sentence. It has a subject, verb, noun, pronoun, etc. Sometimes when we say no to people we love and are in a relationship with, they will ask, "What do you mean by no?" To which I will say, "What is it about no that you don't understand?" Here we go; no means no—that's what no means!

All of my identity cannot be in my wife simply because we are in a love relationship. My identity is as important as hers; hers is as important as mine. We are all individuals. Sometimes a mate thinks he or she should share the spouse's friends because of fear or jealousy. The mate assumes that failure to share the partner's friends may cause the partner to feel that the spouse is not fully committed.

However, the inability of a spouse to have his or her own friends reveals the person's lack of boundaries. The partner who senses this lack of boundaries may then feel, "I am in prison with this mate. I can't breathe." He or she may seek distance and space as a result.

It is possible for your wife to have a girlfriend who does not negatively influence her. Wives, it is also possible that your husband can have male friends who do not negatively influence him. As a matter of fact, I encourage men to develop strong male friendships. Men won't turn homosexual when they get together. They don't necessarily get together to swap girlfriends either. Though all these negative things are possible and do exist, we as Christians can't allow fear to prevent us from godly living.

Selfishness

Because of sin, we are inherently selfish. We seek our own welfare above that of others. We focus our efforts on our personal goals and are consumed by our own interests. By nature, we evaluate relationships based on benefits that we gain from them. If we acquire nothing—materially, socially, or emotionally—from interaction with a person, group, or organization, we tend to avoid getting involved.

I often see this basic selfishness expressed in the misery of some adults who have not yet found the "right" person as a mate. If asked for a description of that person, the single gives answers that reveal a desire to gain from a relationship rather than to give. Rarely are they looking for someone they can reinforce, someone whose interests they can encourage, or someone with goals they can support. Responses from women are more likely to describe someone who is financially stable, with a nice home and a fine car. Men often describe a woman who looks good and who can financially contribute to the relationship.

God directs the Christian relationship to be different. He has given a definitive insignia of relationship that follows His design. That emblem is love—love that seeks the good of others above our own. Love that seeks involvement in the interests of others. Love that seeks to edify another without expecting anything in return.

The essence of brotherly love is that it seeks the welfare of another instead of one's own. Philippians 2:3-4 tells us to do nothing out of selfishness or merely to look after our own interests, but everyone should express interest in the concerns of others. Adlerian psychology restates these biblical truths by defining a well-adjusted human being as one who is interested in the concerns of others, not just the interests of oneself. In order to become concerned with the pursuits of others, we must respect and accept them. We must consider their concerns as legitimate and worthy of attention. By providing positive confirmation of others, we acknowledge their contribution to life, and we enhance their self-esteem.

Anyone who considers only himself will never experience relationships that bring a high level of satisfaction. This person's relationships are prone to sour because of the focus on his own desires. To be able to fully receive joy in life, one must be able to share in the lives of others. There must be a desire to extend oneself. If fulfilling relationships are to be attained, a person must not only consider what he or she receives from the other person, but also consider what he or she can give.

An examination of the reasons for broken relationships will reveal selfishness to be the primary cause. Increasing divorce rates attest that in many circumstances the parties involved are not concerned with the effect of their actions on others, do not care about the effect their disregard has on the spouse, and are indifferent to the repercussions of their decisions on other family members. The result is the laceration of a union that has been formed by God.

Other societal ills also have roots in the inherent selfishness of people. For example, the embrace of abortion and the increase in racial violence are additional legacies of the price we pay for exalting our own desires above what is best for others. Because God intends for people to be concerned about others, those who are selfish will act in a manner that not only harms themselves but leaves casualties among their family, friends, and society.

During a counseling session several months ago, a man expressed the frustration he was experiencing in his marriage. He listed several things he believed he contributed to the relationship, after which he questioned, "What is in this marriage for me?" In response I suggested he change his perspective of marriage to, "What can I give to my mate?" Marriage is often considered a fifty-fifty relationship; however, I would suggest that people in marriages and other relationships need to be willing to give 100 percent to the relationship.

Another area in marriage relationships in which selfishness can deal a deadly blow to fulfillment is in sexual expression between husband and wife. The key word here is participation. Oftentimes the husband or wife will withdraw and refuse to participate. A relationship where one person carries the load usually is not fulfilling. This is evident when husbands say to me in a session that during sexual relations with their spouses, they feel she is just there, not participating, and they will add, "And that's not fun." Of course, the wives always say they know the difference between love-induced sex and selfish sex and that selfish sex doesn't fulfill their sexual needs.

It is important for marriage partners to realize that sexuality is not merely for self-gratification. I am concerned about the women who express the hurt they feel when their husbands do not romance them. For these women, sex is only a matter of satisfying the demands of an insensitive mate. They tell me that they feel as if a rape has occurred. Instead of drawing close to their husbands, they experience anger, resentment, and rage. Seeing no choice but to comply, they sink into hopelessness and helplessness.

It would not be so bad if our selfish desires affected only ourselves. However, that is never the case. What a shame to use selfishly the wonderful gift of life God has given us. When our view of association with others does not include their edification, we limit the possibility for personal enrichment. Additionally, when we resist loving our mate, our children, or others with whom we relate, we invite destruction. Loneliness, alienation, and depression are painful consequences of a lack of concern for others.

God's instruction is that we "give, and it will be given to you. A good measure, pressed down, shaken together and running over" (Luke 6:38). In His infinite wisdom, God could have taught us to hoard the things we have. But that is not how He chooses to bless us. In our relationships, God wants us to remember that we are simply channels of His blessings. He gives to us that we may share with others. In our walk with Him, He wants us to be a reflection of His generosity.

Refusal to Submit

One of the most misrepresented, misinterpreted, miscommunicated, and misunderstood principles in Scripture is that of submission. The order to submit has to be the most detested command in God's repertoire. Submission goes against the grain of every human being. After all, each of us is born with the natural philosophy expressed eloquently by the Isley Brothers: "It's your thing; do what you want to do." If we all received the time, space, and authority to be leaders in our own way, we would be absorbed in our power-hungry agenda before anyone could bat an eye. Let's face it, power feels good! It's fun to be in control.

Just think—someone goes when you say go and comes when

you say come; someone waits on you hand and foot, joyously fulfilling your every desire while sacrificing attention to his or her own
needs. What a perfect picture of submission, right? Wrong! However,
the picture just painted is precisely the image most people get when
they hear the word *submission*.

Though much has been said, and many books have been written on the subject of submission, it is still a matter of great contro-
versy in the Christian community. I will say again, it is one of the most
misunderstood and misinterpreted principles in the Word of God.
Some define submission as total denial of one's dignity, total acquiescence to the will of another—an attitude that says, "You have my
permission to walk all over me in spiked shoes!" Women, in particular, cringe at the concept of submission because for so long men have
used it as an excuse for practicing insensitive, dictatorial, and
ungodly leadership.

Popular myths about submission include the belief that the
Bible commands total passivity in the role of the wife. In the minds
of many Christian wives, the meaning of submission is summed up
during the marriage ceremony in the word *obey*. At that point in the
ceremony, their hearts sank when they were asked if they promised
to "love, honor, and obey" their new spouse. For most, the very use
of the word *obey* means that as a child responds to the commands of
a parent, so must the wife respond to the wishes of her husband—no
question, no comment. Under the guise of submission, wives have
not set proper boundaries and protected themselves against degrad-
ing actions but have subjected themselves to physical, mental, and
emotional abuse. With the attitude espoused in a familiar commer-
cial, women believe they are to listen to their husbands' commands
and "just do it."

For many believers, the concept of submission causes mixed
emotions. They desire to act on God's command to submit, but they

fear possible mistreatment. As a speaker at many women's retreats, I know the emotion evoked by the mention of the topic.

Myths about submission also occur in the workplace. Some Christian workers believe that God expects employees to be nonassertive and timorously compliant. Misinterpretation of the concept as it applies to the work environment leads one to be close-mouthed against unjust, unfair, and unethical business practices. At times believers have been caught engaging in illegal activities after disengaging their biblical filters simply because their superior requested the particular action. Never mind that the activity was shady or suspect. Since, according to faulty reasoning, the apostle Paul admonished servants to obey their masters, the voice of opposition within the conscience that reveals the true sentiment of the Holy Spirit is quenched. Some Christians even believe that the Bible commands absolute acquiescence, almost slavery, in the workplace.

Distortion of God's principle of submission has left many church members victim to unfaithful, unworthy leadership. In some churches leaders live blatantly ungodly lifestyles, yet believers turn their heads because they think that to question the behavior would be to step outside of one's place. As a result, scandalous actions have been perpetrated against congregations—making some of the weaker lambs in God's flock vulnerable to wolves in sheep's clothing.

Lack of understanding of the concept of submission has caused one of God's most basic principles to receive a bad rap even in the Christian community. Though Scripture tells us to submit to government, to employers, to one another, and wives to husbands, the failures of these leaders are cited as a cause to disregard God's directive.

The current attitude regarding submission is shameful, for when we actually look into the history of the word, we see a concept that can best be expressed in a military context. In each military organization, there is a general. This general is not autonomous but receives the command from yet a higher authority. The officer under the general's authority has the same power the general has—rifles, grenades, tanks, etc. The general has the responsibility of communicating the orders received to the officers under his chain of command. It is the responsibility of each officer to listen to the directives of the general, ask pertinent questions, give pertinent information to make the mission a success, and then give 150 percent to the accomplishment of the mission.

Because the officer is acting in concert with the general's directives does not make him or her less of a person. It does not mean that the officer is weak or stupid. In fact, the officer has an extremely important role in the scheme of the organization—the responsibility to direct the soldiers, armory, tanks, and other resources in the accomplishment of the overall goal.

If the officer chose to use his or her firepower against the general, that officer would not only be working against the stated objectives and hinder the successful accomplishment of the mission, he or she would also be tried for treason. It is not just a recommendation, but the responsibility of every person in uniform to perform under the directives of the commander in charge. Despite their own personal opinions about the military strategy, for the purpose of winning a victory, all must submit to the authority over them. Otherwise there would be one million chiefs and no Indians.

Submission is a choice. But it is a choice each of us has the responsibility to make. Submission is different from obedience. God commands children to obey. He does not command adults to obey one another. But for the purpose of unity, he tells us to submit to one another. The Ephesians 5 passage that many men quote to support their view of submission does not really begin with verse 22. It actually starts in verse 21 where Paul encourages both husband and wife to submit to each other.

What is God asking of us when He tells us to submit? What are we supposed to be doing? Our twentieth-century definition of submission, provided by one dictionary, is to "give over or leave to the judgment or approval of someone else." The *American Heritage Dictionary* defines submission as "the act of allowing oneself to be under the power or authority of another." It is a hard lot, but it is one through which God promises blessings.

It is difficult to speak on the subject of submission, but submission is imperative, since it is one of the most fundamental principles of victorious Christian living. Our heavenly Father is not a God of disorder. He has set up His hierarchy—Christ, man, woman. In the family, the children are under the authority of the parents, the wife is under the authority of her husband, and the husband is under the authority of Christ through the organization of the local church. In the case of single adults, they are under the authority of the church, and the church is under the authority of Christ.

The question that I get most often from wives when speaking on the subject of submission is, "What if I am the most educated, most intelligent, most aggressive, or have the better judgment in the home?" Though posed in the context of the family, this question can be expanded to encompass the workplace or the church.

In keeping with the biblical command for submission, the answer is for the one under authority to let his or her strength become the strength of the one in authority. I tell those who ask me this question, "Sell your ideas to the one in authority. Create what Dale and Dorothy Carnegie call in their best-selling book *How to Win Friends and Influence People* a win-win situation. Go to him and give him the idea. Help him understand. Allow him to catch the vision, and let him become the owner of the vision. If he chooses not to go with your idea, that is okay. You have brought your will in line with the will of God and thus kept open the channel of blessings from Him to your life."

The concept of submission is willingly applied in secular institutions such as the military and corporations because everyone realizes that no one can know everything about everything. So the savvy executive surrounds himself (or herself) with people who can provide expertise in the areas in which he or she is lacking. If a husband is truly godly, he will not be threatened by a wife who is intelligent, has money, is spiritual, and is well-educated. He will see her as his ally. The same can be said of godly church leaders. They will listen to the people committed to their leadership.

The secret to successful submission is to not let our egos get in the way. That is where we go wrong. Seeking to be the ones who receive the accolades and praise, we do not want anyone else to get the credit for our ideas and our work. We take pride in ownership and refuse to share anything for the benefit of another. In other words, selfishness and self-centeredness prevent us from living out the principle of submission. As a result, we suffer.

We forget we are in a battle. This battle is a big one. And because of the disunity caused by the lack of submission and accountability, we get whipped. Remember, Scripture tells us that it is not against flesh and blood (humans), but against angels and principalities in high places (spiritual beings) that we war. We are in a spiritual warfare, and the casualties when we do not operate accordingly are our children, our lives, our homes, our communities, our churches, and even our nations. If we really want to understand the essence of biblical submission, we can look in Paul's letter to the Philippians. There he says: "Do nothing out of selfish ambition or vain conceit, but in humility consider others better than yourselves. Each of you should look not only to your own interests, but also to the interests of others" (Philippians 2:3-4).

As believers, we must be willing to respect and work in concert with God-ordained authority—that is, those who are in positions of authority that have been established by God. He has instituted a chain of command in social structures for the purpose of order and accountability. God has given Christ as the head of the church. Pastors, elders, and deacons are leaders in the local body of believers. The husband is the leader in the home. Parents are in the position of leadership over their children. Governmental rulers are our civic leaders. The employer is the leader in the workplace. The teacher is the leader in the classroom. God is into leadership, and He is the head of all.

God makes His position concerning submission very clear. Romans 13:2 warns us against rebellion. Scripture says that believers who rebel against authority are rebelling against what God has instituted, and they will bring judgment on themselves. We are not told what particular judgment to expect; however, I can guarantee it will cause some distress.

It's hard to submit to someone else. After all, that person is only human. As believers, we tend to feel that no one understands the struggle we are in when we have to acquiesce in painful situations. We want an option when faced with circumstances in which submission does not seem to be to our advantage. Why should a wife be expected to work in concert with a spouse who seems to have no direction? What if the employee could lead better than the manager? Our tax laws are not fair; why act in accordance with them? These are some of the other questions that have arisen during discussions of submission. When we submit, we do so in order to honor God. He gives us the ability to respect and honor the *position* of those in authority even if the persons in those positions may not always be honorable. He blesses our efforts and gives us benefits for choosing His directive over our own will. When we choose not to submit to authority, He permits us to experience the painful consequences of our rebellion. Those consequences can be emotional pain, unattained goals, or broken relationships.

We do not have to consider ourselves trailblazers in the area of submission. The beauty of our position as believers is that we have an example. God Himself, in the person of Jesus Christ, submitted to the will of the Father, subjected Himself to a life of humanity, to unfair legislators, and even to an unjust and painful death through crucifixion so that God's plan of salvation would be accomplished for the reconciliation of humanity to Himself.

> *Your attitude should be the same as that of Christ Jesus: Who, being in very nature God, did not consider equality with God something to be grasped, but made himself nothing, taking the very nature of a servant, being made in human likeness. And being found in appearance as a man, he humbled himself and became obedient to death—even death on a cross! Therefore God exalted him to the highest place and gave him the name that is above every name, that at the name of Jesus every knee should bow, in heaven and on earth and under the earth, and every tongue confess that Jesus Christ is Lord, to the glory of God the Father.*
>
> *—Philippians 2:5-11*

This passage lets us know that we are following in the footsteps of Christ when we choose to subject ourselves to the authority of another and that the blessings to be received as a result of submission are unimaginable. Christ Himself paved the way to submission. We do not have to go it alone.

Refusal to Forgive

The last cause of pain that hinders relationships that I wish to address is the lack of forgiveness. The more I counsel, teach, and assist others in the process toward emotional health and healing, the more I recognize the importance of forgiveness in that process. We wound ourselves emotionally and spiritually when we harbor grudges. These wounds only get deeper when we do not address our unwillingness to forgive. Not only do these sores get deeper, but they spread to other aspects of our lives. Just as a malignant cancer cell left untreated metastasizes, until the entire body is physically defeated, unaddressed unforgiveness attacks our spiritual, emotional, and physical health until we experience paralysis in one or all areas.

Christians are commanded to forgive. Christ, in the model prayer, instructed His disciples to pray that the Father would "forgive us our trespasses as we forgive those who trespass against us." In 2 Corinthians, Paul instructs believers not to come to the communion table before resolving issues with their fellow Christians. Forgiveness in the life of the Christian is important, because it is through forgiveness that we are able to purge ourselves of the desire for revenge. When someone has trespassed against us, it is natural to feel the need for vindication. When someone has done us wrong, someone must pay. That feeling is not far from our heavenly Father's view of wrongdoing. None of us is perfect. All of us have acted independently of God. We have all sinned and missed God's perfect standard. God did not overlook our sin. He demanded recompense for man's unrighteousness. Someone had to pay for the wrong, the sin, of this world. That someone was Christ. Now through Him, we have forgiveness of our sin. As believers, Christ commands us to extend that forgiveness to one another.

Forgiveness is what allows God to have fellowship with us. He provided the sacrifice for our sins through Christ and chose to forgive all who accept the gift of salvation. After contemplating such a marvelous gift, how can we not forgive others? How can we penalize our brothers in Christ when God has gone to such great lengths to bring us into fellowship with Him?

The price that believers pay for unforgiveness is high. We not only lose fellowship with those we fail to forgive, but we also lose fellowship with our Father in heaven. When we are out of fellowship with our heavenly Father, He resists us. His blessings are not conferred on us. By choosing not to forgive, we place ourselves in opposition to God.

The penalty that believers pay for unforgiveness is high, but the penalty that God paid for our forgiveness was much higher. God sent His only Son to die for us (John 3:16). The Bible calls that an act of God's grace because *we* were supposed to die, not Christ (Ephesians 2:8-9). And because of that act of grace, we ought to be ready to extend grace to those who have hurt us. No matter how painful the hurt, it doesn't match the pain Jesus experienced on the cross. In other words, if you have been forgiven, you ought to be forgiving!

Six

Exits

When we experience the pain of rejection or the agony of lone-liness, personal failure, or defeat, we seek ways to lessen the pain. If we do not look to Christ for the healing of our past pain and the present pain we create, we will develop behaviors that help us live with the problem rather than solve it. I have termed these behaviors "exits" because they provide a way for us to avoid confronting those beliefs or situations that cause us pain.

We live in a society and age where people don't want to work for the things they get. We live in a microwave society. We want quick results, and if they are not forthcoming, we seek our own quick, easy way out. The divorce rate is growing because people don't want to work on difficult issues that arise in relationships. When the road gets rough, we either get a good lawyer and file for a divorce, or we choose to remain in the marriage but terminate any real relationship through exits. Exiting is not something unique to laypeople. From the pulpit to the pew, all of us are tempted to dodge pain.

There are two reasons why people use avoidance in dealing with difficult relationships. Most people grew up in homes where parents did not deal with difficult issues. They either stayed in separate rooms, spent time on the phone, watched TV, or read newspapers rather than working together to solve the problem. Of course, if that's how either of your parents handled situations while you were growing up, that's what you know and most likely will repeat.

Other exits people take are hopelessness and helplessness. They use phrases such as, "I have given up," "I don't know what else to do," "Whatever I do or say doesn't seem to be the right thing," "Sometimes I feel that God doesn't hear me," or "It's not worth it anymore." The tendency then is to pretend to be happy and shift their focus to something else. I don't understand how people can function for a long time with such a pretense. I have no peace when I have a conflict with my spouse, regardless of how much TV I watch or how many people I talk to on the phone in an effort to sidetrack the issue. Until I sit down and dialogue and resolve or come to some understanding regarding the situation, I have difficulty proceeding as if all is well. Christians who give in to hopelessness or helplessness are basically not in agreement with the Scripture that says, "With God all things are possible."

Exiting in a relationship is like going AWOL in the midst of battle. We avoid dealing with problems by involving ourselves in activities that will temporarily take our minds off the issues. We think we can ignore the problem, and it will go away. By the time we choose to exit, our hope of resolution through biblical means has vanished. We resort to our own devices to fix the problem.

Satan knows, however, that the more he can cause us to rely on our own methods of dealing with our pain, the greater the likelihood that our reliance on Christ will lessen, and the greater our fall will be. Furthermore, he knows that all he has to do is get us to experience the pleasure of sinful actions (which is what I consider his tactic to be), and he has us in a downward spiral to disaster. The devil will never reveal to us the consequences of our sinful indulgence. He will only allow us to gaze upon the glamour of the bait. After we are hooked, he then revels in our destruction. He whispers in the ears of the person we are avoiding statements such as, "You see, he doesn't even think you are worth his time." In most cases people in these situations quickly buy into such statements, creating another set of problems on top of the ones they are attempting to exit from. People who don't trust God and strike out on their own in times of struggle often choose what they think will bring happiness or an easy way out. If they are honest, they will testify later that they only created double trouble. Let's look at some ways people choose to exit when the going gets tough.

Adultery

During a counseling session, Susan told me a sad story that began because she had wanted the attention of her husband. She had taken him for pastoral counseling, and her pastor told her husband to give her some of his time and attention. The husband told the pastor, "I work two jobs in order to provide for my wife. I just bought her a new car, and I pay for this, and I pay for that in the house. What else does she need?"

The wife's reply was simple: "All that you provide is fine, but it can't replace spending time with you. Honey, I really don't know you, even though we've been married ten years."

The husband seemed unable to understand Susan and did not take the pastor's advice. Believing she was without recourse, Susan looked for some way to dull the pain of being ignored by her husband. In her search for love and acceptance, she succumbed to an extramarital affair. She thought, *If I can't get attention at home, I will get it somewhere else.* When she began to turn to the men on her job, it turned out to be the biggest mistake of her life.

Susan didn't start out looking for an affair. But she didn't realize that it is difficult to prevent a relationship from becoming sexual in nature when two people become emotionally attached. She started paying attention to a coworker (let's call him Joe), sharing her family struggles with him, which, of course, led to a close secret relationship. Before Susan recognized what was happening, she was already emotionally entangled, even addicted to Joe's companionship. Now she had a new battle on her hands—to let go of these overpowering feelings.

Her relationship with Joe produced two pregnancies, which resulted in abortions. Later she divorced her husband and left two children in a confused state, trying to figure out what had happened with Mom and Dad. The guilt of the abortions and divorce caused Susan to seek inpatient treatment, during which time Joe left her.

Homosexuality

When Dave was small, he was introduced to homosexual behavior by an older cousin. The acceptance he received as he participated drew him into the relationship. However, as an adult, he sought to live a Christian life. He knew that homosexuality is wrong, and he sought to live in a way that pleased God. Dave felt the call of God, got counseling, and stopped practicing homosexual behavior. Later he got married, and the couple had a child.

But as Dave and his wife encountered problems in their marriage, he got on the phone with his old boyfriend. He felt he could talk to this man when he couldn't talk to his wife. As he resumed his relationship with the boyfriend, Dave went back into homosexuality.

One day in my office, I asked Dave why he went back to that lifestyle. His reply shocked me. He said, "My wife drove me back to homosexuality."

I asked, "How did she do that?"

Dave said, "She is too perfectionistic, and I can never do anything right. Everything must be right before we have sex, and I am not used to such pressure."

Of course, Dave's homosexuality caused him to lose his church, his wife, and his child—and left his child with soul-troubling questions. How did Dave's exit solve his problem? It didn't. It left his own life and the lives of others in a mess.

Incest

As a pastor, Ty considered himself too spiritual for the kind of struggles he experienced. His wife had been withdrawing sexually as a result of their communication problems. Devotional time together had decreased. Ty wanted relief from the pain of his marriage, and Satan tempted him with the option of divorce. Of course, he knew the Bible did not condone divorce, yet he wanted out. Because he did not want anyone to know what he was going through, he failed to get the help he needed. However, the pain that his pride kept him from divulging drove him to increasingly destructive behavior.

Ty turned his attention toward his stepdaughter, saying to himself, "I am not going to continue fighting with my wife over sex. Neither will I commit adultery with any woman." He decided to have a mental affair with his stepchild, who he thought would not recognize what was happening. He began watching her body movements as she played and peeking at her while she was in the shower. His sin progressed to a sexual desire for her. He believed she was too young to say anything about his sexual advances toward her. Over time with increasing frequency of his advances, an incestuous relationship began.

His lustful behavior eventually broadened beyond the perverse relationship with his stepdaughter. He went to the malls and swimming pools, looking at women and masturbating in public. After months of ungodly involvement with his child and other women he had met at malls and swimming pools, his marriage and family fell apart. To make matters worse, he was arrested and charged with indecency with a minor. He decided to seek Christian counseling. We can see how an attempt to deal with problems inappropriately can create other problems that keep the sick cycle going.

Pornography

Pornography, the silent sexual sin, disrupts many homes today. Because the magazines and movies can be purchased in obscure places and hidden in the home, society considers it an issue of privacy. However, no sin is a private sin. Pornography not only wreaks havoc in the life of the one who temporarily enjoys this form of entertainment but also in the lives of those close to him.

Several years ago, the news that a television evangelist had been caught in adultery with prostitutes rocked the nation. Though many were shocked, what they saw was only the end result of a long-term hidden behavior. This behavior never begins with the after-dark excursions. Rather it starts with magazines, progresses to live-action movies, then to live bodies, and at times to multiple sex partners. People who use pornography as an exit will testify that there is definitely no end to the sickness and that the only real result is broken lives and destroyed relationships. When pornography use grows to an addiction, sexual gratification in a marriage becomes a major issue. When I think of how pornography can kill a relationship, my mind goes to three different cases I dealt with recently.

Mary and Bill had been married for nine months when Mary came to me for help. In one of our sessions, she said, "Dr. Acho, Bill must go." I asked what she meant, and her reply was that she wasn't willing to live with someone whose life was full of deceit. You see, Bill grew up watching porno movies and had become addicted. Shortly after his honeymoon was over, he began encouraging Mary to go to bed, saying he had some work to do on the computer. Knowing that she was a heavy sleeper, Bill would go and get his porno tapes out of the garage where he hid them, put them on, and begin masturbating as he had done prior to the marriage. Because it was an addiction that had not been dealt with, Bill couldn't stop this behavior.

One night his wife woke up at midnight and caught him. Because she loved Bill, Mary offered to go to counseling with him. During the sessions with previous counselors, Bill had made a commitment to stop, which lasted for one month. Then he was back into the behavior again. Thinking something was wrong with her, Mary's self-esteem plunged, and she blamed herself. She sought counseling for the second time in nine months of marriage. Through our work together, Mary was able to see that the problem wasn't her issue; it was her husband's.

The second couple we will call Wendy and Bob. He convinced his wife that since they both had given their lives to Christ at an early age, they had missed out on sex education. They needed to watch porno movies together to help enhance their sex life. Wendy did not know that her husband had engaged in this activity with girlfriends in the past. When she got tired of the movies and suggested to Bob that they stop because they had learned enough, he became angry. He moved to the other bedroom, put a VCR in it, and continued watching. Wendy felt abandoned and alone and separated from her husband. This couple failed to realize that as the creator of sex, God certainly does not need assistance instructing people as to how to incorporate a healthy sex life into their marriage.

The third couple, Jerry and Barb, had a different problem with pornography. The husband was into computer pornography. He argued that he wasn't doing anything wrong since he was not hurting anybody, having an affair, or touching another woman. In one of our sessions, Jerry stated that all men needed to have a similar form of release and pleasure. When his wife requested that he stop, he asked her if she would prefer that he go out with another woman. He argued that the behavior helped him to relax and to deal with stress on his job.

Isolation

How many of us have decided never to speak to someone because of something the person did or said? When relating with others becomes too difficult, we find ways to escape. This method of dealing with painful emotion, avoidance, is used all the time by couples in love relationships. Many who come to me for counseling make statements such as: "We never get anything resolved because he or she shuts down on me whenever we have a disagreement."

One may ask what is wrong with withdrawing when there is an argument. Avoidance seems harmless. There may be nothing wrong with retreating for a while, as long as there is a plan to come together later to deal with the conflict. Sometimes people believe that if they avoid the conflict, after a while it will go away. I hear statements such as, "Time will take care of it." The reality is that time does not take care of most things. You have to deal with them, or they won't change.

I encourage couples to have resolutions in mind regardless of the issue. One of the important things I often suggest to couples in conflict is to make an appointment to discuss the issue. In most cases, as long as both parties know there is a plan to deal with the situation, they can wait. Isolation, if persistent, will develop into dislike, and eventually people will simply not want to be bothered anymore.

Television

Couch potatoes are increasing in our society. The TV and other means of entertainment provide a "safe" escape from the real world and its problems. We spend hours watching the escapades of fictitious families while our own families are in crisis. They are in crisis with regard to understanding what the family's values are. In crisis with regard to setting goals for the family. In crisis with regard to the parents developing a strong sense of identity. In crisis with regard to knowing the biblical guidelines for the family. Children are in crisis because no one seems to have time to help with homework or listen to their concerns.

It's amazing how many families that don't have time for family meetings and brainstorming can describe the inner workings of the Dallas Cowboys organization or what is going to happen next on the "Oprah Winfrey Show" and so on. It is amazing the number of families that have decided to let the TV raise their children. I mean, the TV set has now become one of the pieces of furniture that parents purchase for their newborns. As early as three months, most children are occupied by listening to and eventually watching TV. And we all see the effects in our society.

Many men use this vehicle to take them into a fantasy world of sports. Some people choose to avoid life's issues this way, finding the solitude and entertainment more comfortable. Others adopt the lifestyles and attitudes of the media personalities, only to discover these do not work. People who exit through TV viewing, if honest with themselves, will testify that all TV does is delay dealing with the issue. The problems do not go away even after we've spent many hours avoiding them. I know people who have TVs in every room in the house, including the bedroom (and I don't think TVs belong in the bedroom). People complain to me all the time about how a spouse would rather watch TV than deal with the issues. I have even seen marriages destroyed by inappropriate use of TV. Though TV has its entertainment value, my fear is that we are allowing it to keep us apart from each other and to communicate values and attitudes to our children that we have not had time to process and that may not be a part of our belief system.

Telephone

Another seemingly harmless escape from our problems is the telephone. The majority of my clients who struggle with the tendency to use this escape are women. Husbands will complain about the time their wives spend on the telephone talking with their mothers, their sisters, and their friends. On occasion I have encouraged the men by explaining a woman's need to talk and express herself. Even so, inappropriate use of the telephone destroys the thing most women want to build—relationships. I have had many people tell me they know that the people they are talking to on the phone can't give them the love they are looking for. What they really want is the love and attention of the one key person in their life.

I have also touted the benefits for Christian women to have sisters in Christ with whom they can share ideas and suggestions. However, when the time spent on the telephone becomes a hindrance to the growth and health of the relationship between husband and wife, the telephone has become an exit. We may use the telephone for temporary relief, but we must be careful that it doesn't replace the rebuilding of the broken relationship and that it doesn't become an addiction. In cases where the telephone is used to escape relational problems, the need for expression should be turned toward discussion of the true issues obstructing growth in the relationship.

Addictions

"Just a little drink to calm the nerves"—that was the means Gina used to make it through the problems she was having at home. She began to accompany her friends to the nearest happy hour after work. Her spouse noticed a change in her disposition. He also noticed her increasing dependency on the "little drink." It began with wine and progressed to hard liquor. As time went on, Gina became an alcoholic. Her original problem was marital communication, but now in addition to that, she had to conquer alcoholism. A counselor's intervention helped her work through her problem, but intervention does not occur in time for everyone.

The same kind of reasoning as Gina's lay behind Kevin's decision to drink, but the result was more disastrous for him. His habit began also with "a little drink." Going out for a drink with the fellows gave him the ability to cope, or so he thought. He progressed to hard liquor, then to marijuana, to cocaine, and finally to crack. The time and money he spent satisfying his drug habit consumed him. The road back for him was very long and very hard. Though his fellowship with the Lord may be restored, his other losses may never be recovered—all because he avoided dealing with the pain that relationships bring.

Illegal substances are not the only drugs to which we turn for escape. Many Christians taking prescription drugs are on the road to full-blown drug addiction. Some doctors will prescribe Valium or other nerve-calming medications to aid their stressed-out patients. However, the stressors in life never go away. Often they increase. Problems with a spouse that are not addressed may progress to problems with the children, problems at work, and problems with the neighbors. As the stressors mount, people increase the dosages of their medication. In many cases, the result is a patient unable to deal with life unless he or she is under the influence of drugs.

I am not saying that using prescribed drugs for a condition is wrong. I am saying that running to drugs and eventually depending on them does not solve any problems. That's why I encourage clients with emotional problems who may be taking medication to also stay in counseling. The issue must be resolved through dialogue. Taking a pill daily will not repress the sadness one feels over treatment by a spouse. Failure to deal with the initial stress may mean that a person never gains the ability to fully contribute to relationships.

The Benefit of Conflict

Sinful behavior is pleasurable to "the natural man"—the person living out of the old unredeemed nature. Seeking a quick solution to conflict opens the door to disaster. The Bible tells us there is a way that seems right to people, but in the end it leads to destruction. If we only "knew" the end result of sin, we would not be running to it as we do. Unfortunately, Satan will never reveal the result of sin. His goal is to trap us, and after that, to destroy us. He is accurately described as a roaring lion seeking whom he may devour. Sin initially feels great, but over time, we discover its emptiness. It requires more and more sinful behavior to satisfy us. In the end we find ourselves trapped in a complex web of habits and attitudes that are impossible to break or change without God's help.

It takes time and sacrifice to build a relationship. The process isn't an easy one, but it is well worth the effort. When I think about the things people do to escape pain in relationships, I often reflect upon a plant placed in the soil by a gardener. The roots are placed in a hole and covered with dirt, and water is added. The plant exists in cold, filthy mud. In that substance, however, are the nutrients necessary to promote growth. Over time, the plant takes in the nutrients and grows toward the sun. As the process continues, the plant matures and blossoms.

So it is with each of us. God has allowed conflict to be the unpleasant medium that promotes our growth. The struggles of life provide the obstacles necessary to mature in Christ. As we live and experience pain, yet pursue the Son of God, we blossom—become a picture of Christlikeness.

Seven

Attempts to Fix
the Mess

The truth is that most of us do not function in relationships the way God intends. We operate with a great amount of fear, anger, guilt, and shame. Instead of facing our emotions and dealing with them, we ignore or hide them. We are like the housekeeper who daily picks up her broom, sweeps all the dirt into a pile, and then picks up the edge of the carpet and sweeps the dust under it. Once she considers her daily cleaning completed, she sits back and relaxes, only to do the same thing the following day. After a few weeks of "cleaning" the room, she walks across the carpet, trips on the big lump—the accumulation of dirt—and falls.

So it is with us. We look at our relationships with our spouse, our children, our family, and our friends, and we see problems and lack of fulfillment. In a desperate effort to regain control and enjoy the company of others, we plan romantic getaways with our spouse, plan vacations with our children, organize reunions with our family, and have parties with our friends, seriously thinking that changing the environment alone will change the unhappiness, frustration, and confusion. Or we try to change the environment by buying a new house, thinking that a great big house will bring fulfillment to the family. There are so many unhappy people in those big houses. If you were to investigate through your local police station, you would discover that they frequent the big houses to break up family fights just as often as they are called to small houses.

This past year revealed several big-name celebrities who, though it appeared their marriages were so much in order, were actually on the brink of divorce. We need not be surprised or shocked that the superstars get divorces more often than we average citizens, even though it seems that they have all it takes to make a marriage work. Success, fame, and freedom from financial worries do not necessarily guarantee marital happiness.

You see, we often forget that conflict stems from the heart, and unless the heart is changed, the problems will never be resolved. Proverbs 4:23 encourages us to guard our hearts, for out of the heart flows all the issues of life. These issues include selfishness, greed, hate, murder, adultery, etc., all of which originate in the heart before manifesting themselves in the open.

Don't get me wrong. There's nothing wrong with vacations, family reunions, large houses, or parties with friends. These are wonderful. But a vacation can't change the heart. Large houses don't change behavior. A wise old pastor once said, "If you were to take a pig out of its pen in the country and put it in the White House, it would still want to eat slop."

In marriage relationships, I see this desperation often. When years of pain and disappointment have accumulated, the couple will plan a cruise to rekindle their flame. What they discover upon return, however, is that the pain they left is still there. The attitudes they hoped would go away creep back and are just as destructive to the relationship as they were before. The reason is that the people who went on the ten-thousand-mile journey are the same people who came back. The smell of the ocean, the beautiful landscape, and the taste of exotic cuisine do not change behavior.

A client once told me that he thought losing weight would be the key to happiness, peace, and fulfillment in marriage. After running many miles and exercising consistently, he did lose weight, only to discover that nothing changed in his marriage. This client's attitude toward behavioral change is representative of many. They believe that if they could only stop smoking, stop drinking, lose weight, help out more around the house, buy the spouse nicer things, etc., their relationships would get better.

Again, don't get me wrong. Those actions may help, but these changes alone are not the answer. In most cases, they are like New Year's resolutions—you make them today and forget them tomorrow. Since day one, man has attempted to fix his own mess. While the effort is often sincere, the tools used often come from the wrong tool box.

The repair of damaged relationships must begin with God. There is no other solution. God not only created our relationships, but He also created our lives! We quote the passage of Scripture that says, "Therefore what God has joined together, let man not separate" (Matthew 19:6) as acknowledgment that God put the marriage together. We must remember that the Bible also says, "The LORD God formed the man from the dust of the ground and breathed into his nostrils the breath of life" (Genesis 2:7).

This reminds me of the story of the gentleman who attempted to fix his TV set with a hammer in one hand and a blow torch in the other. Obviously he didn't have a clue about repairing TVs. His best bet was to take it back to the manufacturer. Many of us look just as ridiculous when we attempt to fix the mess in our lives and particularly in our relationships. We try to use the instruments we see on TV. We model ourselves after the TV families. If these methods don't work, we follow the examples of our friends' or parents' marriages. We fail to realize that what worked for our friends or parents may not necessarily work for us. We too have the wrong tools, and it's our best bet to take what needs to be repaired back to our Manufacturer.

Our feeble attempts at fixing the messes we make, instead of eradicating the destructive hindrances to growth, only compound the pain. They increase expectations for change when, in fact, the real issues behind the disastrous behavior have not been addressed.

In a final attempt to better the situation, couples may then seek counseling, sometimes thinking that the counselor has a magical power to change their situation. Years ago a suicidal patient in the hospital said to me, "Dr. Acho, if you don't do anything to help me, I will kill myself. Doc, you are my last resort."

I responded, "I appreciate your confidence in me, but I can't stop you from killing yourself. You are the only one who can do that." I proceeded to help him see other options than suicide.

My point again goes back to Proverbs 4:23. We need to watch over, or literally guard, our hearts. Individuals are responsible for what's going on in their hearts. Counseling can help, but the ultimate decision to get well resides in the individual.

Another of my clients told me that counseling was the last step before a divorce. Because of the difficulties he and his wife were having, he did not believe the counseling would actually result in positive change. His reason for coming for counseling was to satisfy his conscience, so if it did not work, he could say he gave it a try. In fact, he verbalized that position, saying he and his wife had decided to give it a try, but if it did not work, he was filing for a divorce.

Sometimes people do not realize that while godly counseling can be very helpful, the counselees may focus more on the process and fail to look honestly at their own shortcomings that call for change. A lot of people get carried away in the counseling process.

Though it may seem strange that one would approach marital counseling with the attitude of the client I just mentioned, his stance is not unique. Many acquiesce to working with a counselor while contemplating the contingency plan after the sessions do not work. Counseling is good as long as the couple has resolution in mind. The effectiveness of counseling sessions is directly proportional to people's commitment to allow the power of the Holy Spirit to work in their lives.

Singles experience the "under-the-carpet" syndrome as well. By neglecting to address issues that cause pain in relationships with friends, family, other believers, and coworkers, they become powder kegs, ready to explode when just the right "match" is struck. Singles, however, have a another escape hatch, particularly in dating. When singles want to avoid addressing issues that cause pain, they trade in their "problematic" relationship for a "new and improved" one. I call it the "switch-partner" method of dealing with issues of the heart. My single clients say, "I'm not committed to him/her yet. Therefore, why deal with this? I'll just run and find somebody else." Most of the salvaging needed in premarital counseling results from the failure to resolve conflict and address the issues that cause pain.

A man came to me who said he was running out of women to date in his small community. I found out that in his effort to find Mrs. Right, he had dated almost every girl in his town. Of course, he never considered that he might change a few things about himself. His idea was that there was a girl out there who "had it" and could fix it all. This kind of thinking clouds the decision-making of many singles.

I know several young ladies who think that if they could only marry a seminarian or a pastor, everything would be perfect. I mean, what could be wrong with anyone who has such a vast knowledge of Scripture? Little do they know that marrying a church leader could land them in as messed-up a situation as marrying anyone else. I know both pastors and seminarians whose marriages are on the rocks! None of us is exempt. In fact, pastors and seminarians seem to have a greater struggle with denial than other people. They have more pressure to appear as though everything is all right. Many of them are like those swans on the lake. As we see them above water, they look proud, breast out as if they have it all together. But if we were to look under the water, they are paddling a hundred miles an hour just to stay afloat. Marital happiness comes not from our circumstances, not from the quality of our mates, but only from the personhood of Jesus Christ.

Think with me for a moment through the following story. Once there was a kid named Johnny who claimed his independence at age twelve. Johnny decided that he no longer needed to depend on his mother and father and that he would take off on his own. He thanked his mom and dad for taking care of him, clothing him, feeding him, and helping him get through school. After this expression of gratitude, he bounced his suitcase down the stairs and took off for the unknown.

If you were to run into Johnny two weeks later, what would you see? Among many other things, you would notice that he's dirty, scared, and hungry. The cold world, in just two weeks, would have had a field day with him. Now suppose you had the chance to give one bit of advice to Johnny. What would you say? Would you tell him to go take a bath? Certainly he would need one. Would you tell him to stop being afraid? Certainly he would need to do that. Or would you prepare Johnny a nice dinner, feed him, and then send him on his way? Certainly he would need that, too.

While those things would meet a temporary need in Johnny's life, they offer little in the way of a lasting solution to his predicament. The only advice that would make a lasting difference in Johnny's life would be: "Go back home!" The fact that he is dirty, scared, and hungry is only evidence that there's no guardian or parent watching over Johnny's life. Those obvious needs are only symptoms or indicators that point to a deeper need. He needs to be brought back into a relationship with his parents to make his life work.

The same is so for us. As I mentioned earlier, Adam claimed his independence in the Garden of Eden. Ever since that time, people have been trying to put the pieces of life's puzzle back together on their own. For example, broken relationships, infidelity, alcoholism, and abuse are all evidence of our need to turn to our heavenly Father to make our lives work. While the world says, "Exercise—that'll fix it," "Take a vacation—that'll fix it," or "Do this and take that and go there, and it'll all work out," what we really need to do is take the same advice that would work for young Johnny. We need to "go back home"—go back to dependence upon our Creator, who knows us better than we know ourselves. He can fix our mess. That's where a God-fearing Christian counselor comes in. Such a person understands the principles of God's Word and knows how to apply them to meet human needs.

We were not created to fix our own problems. All of us have limited capabilities. We can only do so much to rectify the pain in our lives. The truth is that we were created to be constantly dependent upon an all-loving, all-caring God. We were not created to be self-sufficient.

Part Three

Putting the Pieces Back Together

Eight

There's Hope in the House

We've seen how our lives can shatter into scattered fragments, until they become like a disassembled puzzle. It's now time to begin putting the pieces of the puzzle back together. The first step of that process is to believe that there is hope for recovery.

The number one reason people give up and never recover from their brokenness is that they never settle the issue of whether it is possible to recover. Many become so defeated when their worlds shatter that they lose hope for restoration. This loss of hope raises three basic questions. First, what difference does it make to have hope? Second, where do we find hope? And third, once we find where it is, how do we experience it in our hopeless situation?

To illustrate the difference hope makes, consider the following experiment. A scientist, while experimenting with some rats, discovered the energy and power that just a little bit of hope can provide. He had taken several rats and put them in water to see how long they could swim. After about five hours, the rats began to slow down and give up. Just before the rats were about to drown, the scientist took them out of the water, fed them, let them rest, and helped them regain their strength. Then he placed them back in the water to repeat the same experiment. This time the rats swam for thirty-five hours—seven times longer than they did the first time. Why did the rats swim so much longer the second time? The reason was because, unlike the first time, there was the element of hope. The rats knew that because they had been rescued before, there was the possibility that they might be rescued again. That possibility provided hope.

Hope can motivate when everything else seems to malfunction. Hope can help you hang in there even in the most horrible situation. Hope can energize you when all energy is gone. The hope those rats had energized them, motivated them, enabled them to hang in there and swim seven times longer than they normally could have.

Now those of us who are believers have a much greater hope than the mere prospect of survival. Unlike generations before Calvary, we know that when we were marching down a road that said "no outlet," when we were in the worst situation we ever could be, Christ rescued us. Romans 5:8 says that "God demonstrates his own love for us in this: While we were still sinners, Christ died for us." Christ has rescued us out of the most dangerous situation possible. Surely He can rescue a hopeless marriage. Surely He can restore broken hearts. Surely He can cause the breath of life to enter relationships that died years ago. There's hope in the house! Hope that Christ can repair our shattered worlds. Hope that whenever our lives become broken into many pieces and scattered everywhere, Christ can put the pieces back together again. He's able, and, therefore, there is hope.

So what difference does hope make? Hope makes all the difference in the world because some lives are so shattered that the restoration process will take much time. Waiting and going through that process will require endurance and patience. We will have to hold on until deliverance comes. God may have us swim seven times longer before He intervenes. The neat thing about having hope is that, if God requires swimming seven times longer, hope helps us hang on. Having been rescued before from something much worse, we now know we can be rescued again. Thus, we gain strength from the possibility and expectation of Christ's intervention.

We know the difference hope can make. We're convinced that hope helps. The question we need answered now is: "Where do we locate this hope?"

The fact of the matter is that everyone is looking for hope. Hope not only drives the hopeless to hang on in tough situations, but even people who are on top of their circumstances know the incredible effect of hope, and they want it too. This is the reason so many in their search for hope turn to the false hopes that the world offers. Every day people buy into all kinds of schemes to gain a false hope. Unfortunately, they lack the spiritual discernment to detect the fakes.

We see these false hopes at work when a young businessman fresh out of college goes into tremendous debt buying a $65,000 sports car because he thinks such an investment will reap the returns of respect and admiration from his colleagues. He also has been duped into thinking that the car will somehow be instrumental in his finding the right partner for life. His hopes of finding a mate are built on the false hope that an expensive automobile can win a quality woman.

The problem with false hope is that, while it can provide the same motivation and energy that true hope can, false hope leads to an insatiable expectancy. In other words, someone who has a false hope never has his or her expectations fully met. At best, these expectations may be met temporarily. The reason for this is that false hope is circumstantial. We all know that circumstances change often. If a person's hope is based in their circumstances, then as soon as their circumstances change, their hope does too. False hope leaves a person unable to experience contentment in life.

Unlike false hope, true hope produces both peace and contentment. Why? Because true hope has as its basis the Lord Jesus Christ, who, according to Scripture, never changes. Thus, if our hope is lodged in Him and His promises, our hope can be constant and unwavering. Not only is Christ always the same, but He's also sovereign, which simply means He's in full and complete control of our circumstances.

Since we're talking about true hope, and since there is only one source of true hope, the natural place, the safest place, to locate true hope has to be in God. By saying "in God," I actually mean three things: 1) in everything He said about Himself; 2) in everything He said about life; and 3) in everything He said about life to come.

From Genesis to Revelation God has revealed how He has intervened in human affairs to offer true hope. Since the beginning of time, men and women in every walk of life have searched for and found hope in the only true God. That hope caused these people to gain renewed strength and perseverance—strength that caused them to hang on throughout the toughest of times. While we cannot take an exhaustive look at the examples in Scripture of men and women finding hope in God, I do want to examine two instances.

A prophet by the name of Ezekiel raised the question of where to find hope hundreds of years ago when he and the whole house of Israel got themselves into a desperate situation. Their inability to live up to God's standards and refusal to obey Him had brought them a severe punishment. God allowed the Babylonians to take their entire nation captive.

Do you know what it's like to be in captivity? The Israelites were in a hopeless situation. Some of us are just like those Israelites. We have a few Babylonians in our lives. Some of us have been taken captive by the enemy—by low self-esteem, by out-of-control passions, by drugs, by alcohol, by laziness and procrastination and victimization.

And let me drop a word here for you victims—check and make sure that it isn't your fault you're in a hopeless situation before you begin to blame God, blame the white man, blame Mama, Daddy, or your spouse. God allowed the hopelessness to come upon Israel as a result of their own disobedience. Ezekiel 36:17 says that the house of Israel was living on their own land and defiling it by their ways and their deeds and their impurity. It wasn't another nation's fault; it was their own! God said, "According to their ways and their deeds, I judged them!" Could it be that God is judging our society? Why will a man continue in adultery even when he knows he'll destroy his marriage?

A closer examination of this text reveals four things about Ezekiel that caused him to have hope in his hopeless situation. Ezekiel found hope when the hand of the Lord came upon him (Ezekiel 37:1). Sometimes hopelessness can cause life to seem like a big jigsaw puzzle where it's difficult to know which piece goes next. If you don't know Jesus, accepting Him as your Savior is the next piece to the puzzle.

Ezekiel was one of God's own. In fact, the nation of Israel was God's chosen people. But because of their disobedience, God had allowed them to be deprived of their land, deprived of their king, and deprived of their temple. Israel, remember, was a nation without hope. She had been divided and dispersed for so long that unification and restoration seemed impossible. Israel had virtually died in the flames of Babylon's attack.

But when the hand of the Lord is upon your life, there's hope in the house. You see, though God had judged Israel, He also had promised them restoration. Regardless of what He may allow in your life, He always has a restoration plan. Why? So His name might be glorified. Restoration for the nations of the world is on the way—if we meet certain conditions. Second Chronicles 7:14 says, "If my people, who are called by my name, will humble themselves and pray and seek my face and turn from their wicked ways, then will I hear from heaven and will forgive their sin and will heal their land."

Just as parents punish their children's misbehavior in order that they may grow up to be men and women of character, so God corrects His people's misdeeds. When the hand of the Lord is on a life, judgment on sin becomes part of a process of developing character and glorifying God. Judgment becomes the means to an end rather than the end itself. When God's hand is on a life, the end, no matter what happens in the process, glorifies the Lord. Israel, with their ways and their deeds, had gotten themselves into a mess. But the hand of the Lord was upon them, and God turned their situation into a blessing.

Ezekiel 36:33 speaks to Israel in their hopeless situation: "'This is what the Sovereign LORD says: On the day I cleanse you from all your sins, I will resettle your towns, and the ruins will be rebuilt. The desolate land will be cultivated instead of lying desolate in the sight of all who pass through it. They will say, "This land that was laid waste has become like the garden of Eden; the cities that were lying in ruins, desolate and destroyed, are now fortified and inhabited." Then the nations around you that remain will know that I the LORD have rebuilt what was destroyed and have replanted what was desolate. I the LORD have spoken, and I will do it.'" Why will the Lord do all of this? Look at the end of verse 38: "Then they will know that I am the LORD."

Ezekiel found hope when the word of the Lord came to him. Verse 3 of chapter 37 says, "And He said to me." In fact, all throughout the book of Ezekiel, from chapter 1 through chapter 48, Ezekiel says, "And the word of the Lord came to me." However, Ezekiel and most of the Israelites doubted God's promise of restoration. What was the problem? Their present circumstances didn't look very hopeful. You see, it's one thing to believe God when you are in a land full of milk and honey, but when your situation is hopeless, that's a whole different story. Ezekiel doubted God while in captivity. But he doubted only for a little while. He doubted God until the word of the Lord came to him.

Let's examine further to see what happens to a man or woman when the word of the Lord comes. The psalmist said that the word of the Lord was "a lamp unto my feet and a light unto my path." In David's time, a soldier would literally tie a lantern to his sandals as he walked in the night, and every step would light up his path just enough to see to take the next step. This is how the Word of the Lord operates in the life of an individual upon whom God has laid His hand. The psalmist was saying that the Word of the Lord provides direction or gives vision. The word of a pastor can provide temporary encouragement, and soon it fades from the memory. The words of a counselor can provide only temporary encouragement. But God's Word provides permanent direction. And when you find direction, you've found hope.

Notice that not only did the word come to Ezekiel, but God told Ezekiel to use the word to speak life to his hopeless situation. The word not only gave direction to Ezekiel, but brought inspiration and a promise of restoration to the entire nation. Ezekiel found hope in the word of the Lord.

All we've covered thus far is what caused Ezekiel to find hope. He found hope when God's hand was upon him. He found hope when the word of the Lord came to him. But you know what? Finding hope and experiencing hope are two different things. You can find something or know where something is, and it still may not become part of your experience. Many people know where to find love, but locating love and experiencing love are two different things.

This summer we are conducting wedding ceremonies all over the place, but the rate at which people are getting married is also the rate at which divorces are occurring. To me, it doesn't look as if there is any difference between what we do and what the unsaved do. Paul dealt with a similar situation in 1 Corinthians 3. There he said to those at Corinth, "You are still living like mere men." When he said "mere men," he was referring to the natural (unsaved) man he had mentioned in 1 Corinthians 2:14. It was as if Paul was saying to them, "You guys have been saved for several years now. What has changed in your lives?" We need to constantly ask ourselves the same question. When are we going to stop hurting each other in our relationships with one another? When will that change? I don't know about you, but I don't want just to locate hope; I want to have hope. I want hope to be part of my experience. To find hope and not experience it is like having no hope at all.

Ezekiel began to experience hope when he developed a dialogue with the Lord. Verse 3 records the Lord saying to Ezekiel, "Son of man, can these bones live?" But it also says Ezekiel answered! Ezekiel's response to God was, "O Sovereign LORD, you alone know." Notice that in order for Ezekiel to have dialogue with God, he had to be in fellowship with God. In other words, the Bible says that God not only spoke to Ezekiel, but God spoke with Ezekiel. You see, there's a difference. Speaking with someone implies that both parties are active in sharing one with the other. Do you realize that God chooses not to speak to some folk, even though they are His children? Psalm 66:18, says, "If we regard iniquity in our hearts, the Lord will not hear us." When we sin, we offend God, and although our relationship is not affected, our fellowship with Him is interrupted.

You don't experience hope until you are living in harmony with God. Ezekiel developed a dialogue with God when he complied with the commands of the Lord. When God told Ezekiel to prophesy, Ezekiel prophesied—whether it was to dried-up bones or to the whole house of Israel. When God told Ezekiel to do something, he didn't ask God why; he did it. You see the promise wasn't automatic.

God said to Ezekiel, "Prophesy, and . . ." The promise provided hope, but Ezekiel had to obey the Lord's command. I don't believe Ezekiel would have experienced hope had he not prophesied.

I don't know about you, but it looks kind of foolish to me to prophesy to some dried-up dead bones. But sometimes God wants us just to trust Him. For God to restore Israel seemed as incredible as for Him to cause dry bones to become living human beings again. The thing I like about Ezekiel is that this prophet knew that the fulfillment of God's promises depended upon God, not on circumstances.

Can we say that today? How many of us today are looking at our circumstances, or how many of us have our eyes on the Lord? As Christians, we all know and have heard over and over the promises of God. We sing Sunday after Sunday that He'll bring us out, He'll make a way out of no way. But first we need to ask ourselves, "Have we complied with the Lord's commands?"

It may look foolish for you to stoop and serve your spouse. But you need to trust Him. It may be hard for you to give up trying to have the last word. But you need to trust Him. It may look foolish for you to stay pure until you're married. But you need to trust Him. What is God telling you to do today? Are your eyes on the Lord, or are they on your circumstances? You better go ahead and obey the Lord. Ezekiel says in verse 7, "So I prophesied as I was commanded." What is God commanding you to do?

I realize that some of you can say, in the words of the great poet Langston Hughes, that life for you just "ain't been no crystal stair." The road you've traveled has led through some tacky situations. I'm writing today to tell you not to let go. You need to hang in there. No matter how hopeless your situation is, there's hope in the house!

If you place this book down with clarity in your mind that you've got the hand of the Lord upon your life, and you're going to allow Him to place you in a position where the Word of the Lord can come to you, and you're going to maintain fellowship with Him by developing and maintaining a dialogue with Him, and you're willing to comply with His commands—then you have every reason to hope!

Nine

Treating Spiritual Amnesia

People who suffer from amnesia have lost their identity. They do not know who they are, and they seek clues that will provide a window into self-awareness. They search out people, places, or things that will provide insight about the past. Wandering in a sort of limbo, they are aware of their present existence; however, their tie to their own personal history has been broken.

Spiritual amnesia affects many Christians today. At one time, these believers knew who they were, but somehow they forgot. At one point, they believed in the power of God to keep them pure. They could pray and trust God for answers. They refused to compromise their faith in the workplace, school, friendships, or in the context of their families. At one point, they understood resisting the devil and watching him flee. They understood and experienced the victorious Christian life.

But now the pressures of life and the lifestyles of the unsaved have caused them to forget who they are. These believers can intellectually identify their position in Christ. However, experientially they are not in fellowship with the Spirit of God, and thus they cannot live out of the truth of their position in Him. To fill the vacuum, they begin to search for significance and belonging in things other than God, and they forget that they have received God's divine redemption from eternal destruction. They look to friends, family, and coworkers to lead them through the maze when, in fact, Christ is the one they should follow.

Many of those people to whom the one with amnesia turns are afflicted with amnesia themselves. Like a blind man seeking a black cat in a dark room, the "lost" person trusts these others to know the way to self-fulfillment. Yet most people do not know who they are and have no clue as to who anyone else is either. There is no alternative but to define people based on their behavior, achievements, or family connections, etc. If the people thus defined are not acceptable, rejection occurs.

Rejection is not something new to human society in these last few generations. Rejection began when Lucifer rebelled against God, rejecting divine authority. The tendency to reject has been passed on to us, and we pass it on to others. As we relate, people reject us. As a result, we reject others. We reject others because of skin color. We reject others based on education, on income, on social status, on appearance. We have all been hurt in the rejection game and, as a result, have become master players.

The ideal is to find complete acceptance—to be loved just because we are, not because of anything we do. We seek lifelong partners who will never reject us. We search for friends who will stick by us, come what may. The truth, however, is that our lives will never be that way. There will never be a marriage, a friendship, or any other relationship that does not include rejection at one time or another. I remind myself all the time that the relationships I have with people will one day come to an end, except the one I have with Jesus Christ. The relationship I had with my father came to an end years ago when he died; the one I have with my mother, wife, and children will also come to an end. However, my relationship with Jesus Christ will never cease. It continues forever. This truth helps me keep my focus on the most important relationship of all.

So when I feel rejected in relationships, it hurts, but I refuse to let it get to me. The reason is that God is the only one capable of satisfying our need for complete acceptance. We must keep in mind also that human acceptance is limited. God has placed within our soul a void that only He can fill. He desires to meet our needs. He alone is our sufficiency. Human beings don't have what it takes to meet all the needs of another human; only Christ can meet all of our needs effectively.

If I had earned enough income to provide for all our household budget areas, incidental expenditures, emergencies both seen and unseen, as well as create an excess to give to others, I would say that my job met all my financial needs. If my boss came into my office and said that because of my performance, I will receive an extra five thousand dollars in my December paycheck, I would be ecstatic! However, that additional five thousand dollars is only a bonus. I do not have to have it in order to know that my finances are sufficient or complete. It would be great to have the extra money, but all the financial provision I need is in my original salary.

So it is with our relationship in Christ. He has provided all we need in order to make us rich or complete in every way. Because of Christ's suffering, God has restored us to Himself and is providing full acceptance. If, then, my spouse does not tell me what a good job I am doing, that is okay. I would like to hear my mate say that, but compliments are only a bonus. If my boss does not pat me on the back and tell me that I am of value to the organization, that is okay. It would be nice if he said that, but his verbalizing my significance does not determine my self-worth.

All that is needed for love, belonging, complete acceptance, empathy, support, and encouragement is provided in our relation-ship with God. Therefore, the main thrust of attention must be given to developing a relationship with Him according to His standards. Our interaction with others is our relational bonus. That fellowship is not to be pursued in place of our primary fellowship with Christ. There is no relationship more important than our relationship with Him.

Accepted in the Beloved

Before we accepted Christ—before our spiritual emancipation—we were locked into a way of living based on our emotions. Our responses to the situations around us were founded in our feelings. When an event occurred, we would mentally process it based on the information we had received from the various sources that have impacted our lives since birth. That event might cause emotional responses of anger, sadness, or some other negative feeling. These emotions then would lead to certain behaviors—angry words, tears, withdrawal, or depression. We could not draw on the power of God to respond in accordance to His will.

Now that we are alive in Christ, we have the ability to see things differently. We no longer have to act according to the old patterns of behavior we had formed early in life.

Imagine you are driving down the highway at eighty miles per hour. Your radio is turned up until the sound reverberates on the concrete. You are riding high with the top down. You look in your rearview mirror, and suddenly you see red and blue lights flashing on top of a police car.

What emotions do you feel at this moment? Probably fear, anxiety, or sadness. You may begin to perspire or to think about the explanation you will give your spouse. Assume that as the officer closes in on your vehicle, he gets another call to help in a terrible accident ahead of you, and he passes without giving you a ticket. What happens to your previously charged-up emotions? Do you remain in a state of worry, anxiety, and fear? No. Rather you move to a state of relief, joy, excitement, etc.

Prior to knowing Christ, we lived in ungodly ways that had consequences, so we probably deserved the confusion, betrayal, dishonesty, and pain we experienced in our relationships. However, now that we are believers, Satan tries to get us to continue to rely on those ungodly ways of behaving and relating or to fall back into them after we have begun to function in a new way. Christians need to recognize the game of the enemy and fight back. James 1:13-14 provides us with insight, saying, "When tempted, no one should say, 'God is tempting me.' For God cannot be tempted by evil, nor does he tempt anyone; but each one is tempted when, by his own evil desire, he is dragged away and enticed." The knowledge we need to develop good relationships has been offered, the freedom delivered. We must tap into them.

Now that we have been made new in Christ, we are no longer bound to act the way we used to do. We can now look to the simple ABCs of cognitive restructuring, or what the Bible calls renewing our minds. The reason we need to pay attention to our minds is that what we think about ourselves and the events of our lives determines how we will respond and, to a large degree, the success we experience.

I believe that 70 percent or more of the problems in the criminal justice and health care systems today have their roots in faulty thinking. The young man who robs a corner store seeks to gain wealth without working for it. Why does he desire ill-gotten gain to the point of self-destruction? I suggest that somewhere during his development, he received messages that suggested he was not worth much. In order to feel important, he had to have money or material things, and if he couldn't get these the right way or work for them, he could take them from other people. That child never learned to respect other people's property. Somewhere he picked up the idea that someone owed him something, and he must get it through stealing.

A twenty-year-old woman sat in my office one day with tears in her eyes, expressing anger toward her parents. They were well to do, and she had never had to worry about money or do without what she wanted. But when it came time for her to go to college, they told her she was on her own financially, that there was no money for her education. She said, "I wish I had been told exactly how things were at home, rather than being deceived into thinking that we were financially secure when we were not." Unable to handle this new turn of events, she blamed herself and wondered what she had done wrong. Eventually she went into drugs.

In many cases, we have communicated to our children that in order to be acceptable, they have to look a certain way, dress a certain way, and do certain things. In an effort to become the person that they have been programmed to be, they act in a deplorable manner— killing for a pack of cigarettes, for a baseball hat, a can of pop. Sometimes as I read the paper or watch the news, I wonder what has happened to the minds of our young people. We must remember that as a person thinks in his heart, so is he or she.

So many people in jail today would not be there if they had used the mind as it was meant to be used. So many clients tell me that they wouldn't be divorced today if they had thought things through prior to the behavior that led to the divorce. Many of the things we do in counseling are attempts to restructure and help renew the minds of our clients. Sometimes it is difficult for adults to see God's perspective on matters because their minds are basically set in an ungodly perspective. That's why we encourage people with young children to give them the greatest gift of all—aligning their minds with the mind of God. When these children become adults, they will make sound biblical decisions that will be pleasing to God and keep them out of trouble.

Thinking Right

Architectural structures are placed on foundations appropriate for the size of the building. An engineer designing a structure gives much consideration to its foundation. It must be crafted in such a way as to withstand shifts of the earth underneath it, the weight of the edifice on top of it, and the changes in the elements around it. The foundation should be designed to withstand earthquakes or floods. When the building is completely furnished and at full capacity, the foundation should not sink under the pressure. When the wind and rain come, the snow falls, and the sun radiates on the building, the foundation should continue to hold up the edifice.

God places great importance on our spiritual and emotional foundations as well. Jesus told a parable of two men who built houses. One of the men built his house on sand; the other built on rock. When the rain came and the wind blew, the man with the house on sand had a crisis on his hands. But the man who built his house on the rock had a secure home. The house was not secure because of what it was made of; both homes may have been of the finest materials. The home was secure because of its foundation.

God wants us to structure our belief system on Him. He wants us to build on our knowledge of who we are in Him. After we have recognized who we are in Christ, we have a stable foundation, a true measure by which to gauge our actions and reactions. We no longer have to depend on what anybody else says or does to determine how we will respond. We are free to behave in accordance with God's will for our lives.

Satan knows that the most important determinant of people's actions is their belief system. He knows that if we think incorrectly, we will act incorrectly. Therefore, his greatest goal is to cause people to believe a lie. He seduces us into destruction by causing us to adopt a belief system based upon human wisdom and preferences. Humans are fickle creatures. We change our minds based on circumstances. I may think you are ugly and react negatively to you, based on my perception. However, if you gave me three million dollars, my perception would change. My negative reaction may cause you to feel sadness, anger, hatred, or even happiness, and, in turn, you may act on those feelings.

God has designed us to relate with others, but He never wants events to determine how we feel. Circumstances have a tendency to make us feel a certain way, but before we respond in anger, in hatred, in sadness, or even in happiness, we must filter the event through our belief system. That belief system, if grounded in the Word of God, will always provide us what we need to respond in accordance with God's will. We need to reject Satan's lies. He has no hold on us. Scripture tells us that Christ has made us "free indeed" (John 8:36).

As I mentioned earlier, none of us is perfect, and none of us has been born into a perfect world. If you have not yet faced a world-shattering experience, in the words of the old preacher, "keep on living." Chances are, no one will skate through life without encountering such experiences. Thus, it's not a matter of *if* these troubles will come; it's a matter of *when*. And as we saw in the previous chapter, when they occur, the first thing to do is "remember who we are in Christ." It's helpful as well to remember that our old identity before Christ has no bearing on our new identity in Christ. According to 2 Corinthians 5:17, we are a "new creation; the old has gone, the new has come!"

Confronting the Problem

I would suggest that the next piece, as we put together the puzzle of our life, would be to confront our problems head-on! The biggest myth Satan wants us to buy into is that we are already defeated. Nothing can be further from the truth. In fact, Scripture tells us that we are "more than conquerors" in all things (Romans 8:37) through Christ. I pray that the underlying thread through this entire book is that we are victorious in Christ! And in Christ, we can do all things (Philippians 4:13), including draw upon our capacity to confront the problems we encounter in life. Far too many of us give in too easily. We live in a society that is controlled by emotions. "If it feels good, do it. Don't think about it or fight it or reject it. Just do it!" It's time for us to begin to resist these lies, confront them, and experience the victory!

In confronting our problems, I recommend three strategies—simple in application yet profound in results. First, we need to look at life through the lens of God's perspective (John 14:6). What I mean is that we need to make a distinction between how God sees this world and the people in it and how people see this world and themselves. There is a great difference between these two views.

Observing what matters to human beings and what matters to God provides us with a good example. It's clear that people value basically three things in this world. They value beauty, they value brains, and they value bucks. Man, through the media, has for the most part dictated to the world the standards of beauty. When we meet individuals who don't have the high cheek bones, even teeth, or the soft hair of the girls in the commercials and the men in the magazines, we immediately put them down as unattractive. They don't meet the standard.

The world's standards are the major opposition that we as believers have today. I ask myself why it is that we go to church, listen to the Word, and then don't apply it past the church door. The answer is simple. The world's standards and views meet us head-on as we step out the church doors. And we haven't learned what to do with those standards and views.

Again, if you have not been to college or do not have an earned degree, your skills are not marketable in the workplace. And, lastly, if you don't have money and the things money buys, you are not looked upon as a person of value.

For many of us, if you're from the same planet I'm from, the first step in confronting our problems is to reject the world's standards for determining our worth. In rejecting or turning away from worldly standards of success, we turn to and accept God's standards in Jesus Christ. It is because we are His that we are valuable. Just as our paper money, which has no inherent value, is only valuable because it bears our government seal and the picture of one of our presidents, so are we valuable because we bear the image of the God of the universe. Not some of us, but all of us, the entire human race bears that awesome image!

All too often we have allowed the world's standards to shape not only what we think of ourselves, but also how we view other people. I have come across several young singles who, in a search for God's mate for them, have rejected quality candidates only because they did not measure up to those worldly standards—beauty, brains, and bucks. And I've encountered dozens of couples who married because the prospective spouse met all the worldly criteria—not because they had complementary goals for serving the Lord, not because they had similar backgrounds, not because they genuinely loved each other, and not because they were attracted by the other person's love for God.

I'm sorry, but as Christians we can't play ball by the world's rules. Beauty, brains, and bucks are shallow assets, too superficial to use in measuring the worth of human beings created in God's image.

And notice that the world's idea of success does not last. All beauty, intelligence, and wealth are going to burn up one day. The Bible talks about three kinds of fires. Second Corinthians describes a fire that will destroy the works of Christians performed with impure motives. In 2 Peter 3:10-12, there's mention of a fire that will destroy all the elements with intense heat, speaking of the fire that will destroy the world. And finally, in the book of Revelation, we read of a lake of fire into which all the people who never knew the Lord will be cast. Considering these three fires, people who live life according to the rules of the world will only be able to say to one another in the last day, "My pile of ashes is bigger than yours."

Putting on God's Glasses

Many of our problems are mere problems of perspective. Looking at life through the lens of God's perspective first of all means we take ownership in God's value system and reject the value system of the world. Secondly, when people in particular or in society at large condemn us or our culture or background or whatever, the appropriate way to respond is to grasp the information and process it correctly. One of the difficulties with handling our problems is that many of us do not know the correct way to process information that the world sends us. Consider the following approaches.

Let's call the first approach processing information with our human minds. This is the kind of processing the teenage girl uses when she buys into statements from other girls on her campus that she's ugly. Then she begins to behave accordingly, as if she really is ugly. She thinks deeply later on about what that actually means and is convinced that it is true until the most handsome guy in the school asks her to the prom. Her perception of herself depends upon what others think, say, and feel about her.

Now let's apply the second approach to the same scenario. Suppose once the young lady hears the girls say she is ugly, instead of feeling ugly and behaving as though she is, she pauses and thinks through what they said. She tries to activate her own belief system and not depend on others' opinions or on whatever is sending the negative message. As a Christian, her belief system would tell her that she is fearfully and wonderfully made (Psalm 139:14-16). Her belief system would cause her to remember she is made in the image of the almighty God. As she processes and comprehends the information before acting, her own belief system will cause her to reject the negative statements of others. And, of course, she would not be controlled by what someone else says, because she has her own reservoir of Christian truth to dictate her values and beliefs. Any message sent by people or events that doesn't agree with her biblically based belief is rejected and replaced with what matters—her Maker's view of her.

Finally, it's true that life does in fact throw some pretty rough curve balls. When they come, the temptation often is to react rather than respond. When we react, we may jump too quickly. The result may be decisions that we regret later. The best way to handle difficulties and all of life's curve balls is to respond and not react. We respond by going into ourselves and questioning our feelings, looking at what is causing them, and making a decision to act before we react. Taking this approach prevents other people from acquiring power over us. Taking this approach involves our evaluating not only what is being said, but also the source of the information.

We can't allow people to control how we feel. We have a joy in Christ that neither the world nor circumstances gives. So neither the world nor circumstances should be able to take it away. The difference between joy and happiness is that happiness is based on circumstances that will always be changing; thus, happiness will always be changing. On the other hand, our joy is based in an unmovable

God who is the same yesterday, today, and forever (Hebrews 13:8). Thus, our joy will never change.

So let's confront our problems head-on by rejecting the world's values, by processing correctly what the world says to us through comprehending and thinking through it thoroughly before behaving, and by hearing what the Word of God says on the subject. We must evaluate the validity of the source of the information before we believe it. The word *confront* has a negative connotation to many people, suggesting aggression or violence. My definition of it here simply means to think through what is being said and actively reject it if it doesn't apply or accept it if it does. In other words, we are to be in control at all times of what goes into and comes out of our minds. Other people shouldn't make you do anything or refrain from doing it. Your action should be based on your beliefs, and your behavior should be based on the Word of God, not others' worldly opinions. Far too many of us live our lives to please others. "I did this or that because he or she made me" or "Satan made me do it." Such behavior contributes to the destruction of our relationships and cannot go unchallenged.

A Parent's Greatest Legacy

That is why it is so important for parents to instill in their children the principles found in the Word of God. Only by such instruction will they be able to retrieve the truth they need at a later time. The Holy Spirit will only bring out what's already in our minds. John 16:8 informs us that one of the roles of the Holy Spirit is to convict the world of sin. In other words, when people have the Word of God in their minds and hearts, they cannot do anything displeasing to God without experiencing some discomfort.

There was a young man who, prior to becoming a Christian,

dropped by his parents' house every Monday night during the football season to watch football. As he enjoyed the game with his brothers and sisters, he also enjoyed drinking with them and smoking marijuana. Then he became a Christian, and that next football season, he felt uncomfortable about visiting and getting high with his family. The few times he did drop by on Monday nights, his brothers and sisters would hide their beer and marijuana. Why would they do this? He looked no different than he did before. The reason was that now the Holy Spirit had taken up residence in his life. Thus, his mere presence caused everyone in the room to feel uncomfortable. Now I use the word *discomfort*, but the word the Bible uses is *conviction*.

As we hide the Word in the hearts of our children, even while they are in their adolescence, we accomplish two things. We help preserve their young lives by the conviction they will receive from God's Word and the Holy Spirit working in them, and we help preserve the environment in which they live, because the Spirit of God living in them will generate conviction in those around them. God have mercy on those who will remain here on earth after the Rapture when all the Christians are removed. The restraint of evil we now experience by the presence of the Holy Spirit in the lives of believers will then vanish.

Ten

Confronting Our Problems

We have seen the impact of sin on our ability to relate to others. Sinful behavior not only creates problem situations, but it also affects the manner in which we deal with those problems. At the point where we know something is wrong and that our ability to live a fruitful, abundant life has been obstructed, the next option should be to identify and confront our problem. For many of us, it is not hard to identify our problems—that is, if we have made the conscious decision to be truthful with ourselves. The difficulty comes when we must face and confront the problems we identify.

By nature (our sin nature), we seem to choose to do the exact opposite of what God would have us to do. We try to build a so-called satisfying relationship on the pretense that everything is okay when, in fact, a problem has occurred that causes pain. Our state of fallenness encourages us to be nice and pleasing rather than to be honest with ourselves and those around us.

The reason we fall victim to the inability or fear to confront is because our society has given the word *confrontation* a bad name. To be labeled "confrontational" is negative in our "go-along-to-get-along" culture. For that reason, most people strive to maintain the status quo even when something should be said or done to bring wholeness to the situation.

Once in a while women will come to me for advice regarding marrying an African man, wanting my opinion since I was born and raised in Africa. Most of the time, they will express fear because they believe that African men are confrontational and aggressive. They have no problem with the aggressive part, but the confrontational part causes concern. Of course, their question leads me into explaining how Africans confront. From my experience, I know that most Africans are very expressive. They have no problem sharing their feelings with anyone, be these bad or good. Their understanding is that if someone does not like what they are saying or how they are confronting, the listener will speak up. They do not feel that their lives are in danger since most Africans do not carry weapons.

Most Africans believe that a true relationship involves each knowing exactly how the other feels. They believe that true friendship begins after you have confronted and expressed true feelings to one another. During courtship, most Africans will behave their worst with the spouse-to-be. They then say something like: "You have now seen my worst behavior. Do you still want to be involved with me?" So it is a major culture shock when Africans come to the United States and discover that with most people you cannot express those true feelings. You cannot get in someone's face and say exactly how you feel without the danger of being isolated from that person.

Most Africans who marry American women will cease talking loudly because loud talk makes most people nervous, and Africans do not understand why. The African may get into trouble not only in the relationship with a spouse but also with the law because he does not have a problem confronting people in law enforcement either. To Africans, confronting is a way of life.

Lots of clients coming to my office struggle with being honest with each other about their feelings because of fear of rejection or fear of what the other person may say. As a result, we do not deal with anything; rather, we stifle the feelings. These emotions eventually turn into anger, which, if not dealt with, turns into depression. Sometimes the failure to confront each other turns into self-destruction because we also refuse to confront ourselves. We see things we are doing that need to be dealt with, but we will not touch them. Because we are not used to being honest with others, we are not honest with ourselves. I am sure you know people who are aware of some failings, but rather than accepting their weaknesses, they look for a scapegoat, someone who is at fault for their inability to do whatever.

Although our society sees confrontation as a negative, the opposite is true. Confrontation can actually elevate the relationship to a level of deeper intimacy, understanding, and transparency. If the truth be known, confrontation produces far more good than harm. I tell people all the time that we should confront in love because we love. If I do not love you, I never care about confronting you. We call confronting "sharing love with others."

Though we argue that confrontation actually produces positive results, the truth remains that confrontation is not the road we naturally choose. It has been the strategy of Satan from day one to encourage us to pursue the road of least resistance. Certainly choosing to confront someone, particularly someone close to us, is always the road where tension is the greatest. Many have bought into the lie that the greater goal in our relationships is to maintain peace—that keeping things pleasant and always getting along is the true evidence of a growing godly relationship. Nothing is further from the truth. This kind of "pleasant" relationship is unrealistic in a fallen world. Perhaps in a fairy tale, the goal of unending peace would be practical, but in a household where different personalities interact day in and day out, making conflict inevitable, such a goal would constantly cause disappointment.

People sometimes come to me and complain about a lack of love from their spouse. They go on to say that only the people on the job love them and understand them. My response will always be, "Most people on your job don't really love you because they don't know you. They are doing what they were taught to do at work—to be polite, courteous, and kind to all people." The only people who will really show genuine love to you will be people who really know you, i.e., your family. That is not to say that people outside your family cannot love you, but there is a major difference between these two types of love.

Without going into all the psychological details, our fallenness is mainly to blame for our failure to see the positive nature of confrontation. The guilt and separation resulting from the sin nature we inherited from Adam cause us to desperately long for God's acceptance. Though ultimately it is God's acceptance that we really want, that need for acceptance manifests itself in other ways in our relationships with human beings.

Of course, being accepted helps alleviate the guilt and separation that come with our inheritance of a sin nature. This is why we like to be accepted. This is why it is so easy to become people-pleasers. I see this manifested often in the lives of people in ministry by a "save-the-world" mentality. It is almost as if people are trying to win acceptance by making everybody so pleased with them and their actions that no one has any reason to dislike them and, therefore, no reason not to accept them.

In my estimation, this is one of Satan's most crafty devices. The need to have everybody accept and approve of us has caused a lot of harm in many relationships today. I tell people all the time that I would rather worry about Christ's acceptance and love than everybody else's. Christ's acceptance lasts forever. Human acceptance is temporal and based on their feelings and my performance. Since I cannot guarantee

I will perform to everybody's standards at all times, it is therefore a fruitless effort for me to continue to pursue everybody's acceptance.

While the motive driving these people to acquire acceptance may be pure, their method is all wrong. As Christians, we do not seek acceptance by being nice. The need to be nice has left us with little value for honesty. We gain acceptance by receiving what Jesus Christ did on Calvary for us, by being transparent and true to His Word. I think of the hymn, "Jesus Paid It All." We don't have to do anything to win God's love. Whether we confront someone on an issue or not has absolutely nothing to do with our acceptance by God. Furthermore, nowhere does Scripture encourage us to seek after people's acceptance. As Christians, our goal is to rest in the acceptance God gives through His Son and leave the social ramifications to Him.

The negative view of acceptance and confrontation in our society is caused by faulty thinking. To confront someone has meant running the risk of being called a troublemaker. This is particularly so if the other person does not respond well to the confrontation. If the one confronted blows up and creates a scene, witnesses may blame the one doing the confronting for the disturbance.

Whether it be confronting another individual or confronting a personal problem, we have to tackle issues head-on that endanger our relationships. We begin by appreciating fully what Christ has done for us on the cross. Once we understand that nothing, not the problem we are confronting, not the people involved, not even ourselves, can separate us from His love, we will be more willing to confront.

Scripture does not require Christians to be silent when they have been wronged. Jesus Christ told His disciples in Matthew 18 (a passage that many wrongly quote for the purposes of church discipline) how to address a brother when a transgression has occurred. He does not say to sit quietly and lick your wounds because these will eventually heal. Instead, in verse 15, Jesus says we are to go to a brother and tell him if he has offended us. Now initially we are to address our brother alone. And, in keeping with all of Scripture, we must also be sure that our confrontation is done in love. The end of verse 15 says that if the person hears you, you have gained a brother. Again, the preservation of a relationship is stressed. The entire purpose is to win a brother.

Given Christ's instruction, we must conclude that confrontation is not a bad thing. It is a good thing. It is a necessary thing. However, it is for the purpose of building the relationship, not tearing it down. Many will say, "I am going to give him a piece of my mind and then never talk to him anymore." As a result, many have confronted in the wrong way, and they remain enemies for years.

Confrontation will never be easy. Confronting both people and our problems is a skill we might as well learn now, because life is sure to give us the opportunity to confront. It is not a matter of "will we have problems?"; it is a matter of when. Difficulties in relationships with others are a reality for all of us. Thus, confrontation will always be needed.

I believe that our predicaments come in three categories: those that occur as a result of living in a fallen world, those we create, and those we allow others to create for us. Throughout the pages of this book, I have addressed these problems as the reasons for the shattering of our personal worlds. You may have seen your own story in these pages. If your situation was not described in actuality, you may still have seen principles that apply to you. Consequently, I would like to outline some practical steps toward confronting our problems.

The first thing we must do in the journey toward wholeness is to acknowledge the problem. The majority of those who have read the book to this point will understand that something is wrong. There is indeed a problem in your life that needs to be addressed because it is causing pain and preventing emotional and/or spiritual health. The initial step of acknowledging the problem is irrevocable. Unless we admit the problem, we will never face it or deal with it. Acceptance is a difficult stage for many of my clients to get through. Of course, we can acknowledge the need only if we have come out of denial. Acceptance is the opposite of denial. Whether or not we have the capacity to accept is not the issue, for we have no problem acknowledging when things go well. It is only when things go wrong that we try to ignore the difficulty. The best evidence that we have accepted our problem is our willingness to try to resolve it.

A client of mine who was struggling with alcohol told me he had accepted it, but I felt otherwise when he failed to complete an assignment. His problem with alcohol had caused him to lose his family as well as his job. I asked him to get involved in an addiction support group, contract for accountability with a friend, and seek new friends. A week later when I asked about the assignment, he told me he had done nothing. I explained to him that he had acknowledged the problem, as evidenced by his willingness to visit me, but he had not accepted it. It was time for him to move to the next level.

After the problem has been identified, give yourself permission to feel however you may truly feel as you progress in dealing with the problem. Allow yourself time. After all, healing does not occur overnight. Healing is a process.

The next step is to grieve whatever loss you have experienced as a consequence of the problem. People grieve in different ways. But in general, you need to allow the natural feelings of pain, sadness, or a heavy heart to come to the surface rather than repress them. I am reminded of King David when his son was dying (2 Samuel 12). He grieved by putting on sackcloth, fasting, lying all night on the ground, refusing to socialize, staying in a praying mode. He anticipated a miracle from God for his son. But when the son finally died, he started on his road to recovery from his grief. He took a bath, ate, and socialized again, changed his garments, and worshiped the Lord.

In American culture, people grieve differently. Some suppress grief, and some do not. Most men, for example, will stifle their feelings and "act macho," as if it does not hurt. Later they may express it in negative ways—through sexual aggression, punching holes in the walls, hitting their spouses or children, or overindulgence in alcohol or drugs. It is important to realize that if grief is not processed well, it will develop into depression. Sometimes my clients express shock when, after grieving a situation for more than six months, I say to them that I now hear symptoms of depression. So we must now change direction and deal with the pain.

For some the particular problem may be so serious that they have a full awareness of the resulting suffering. Others may engage in a strong denial that prevents acknowledgment of this pain. People should not be ashamed of feeling pain when they experience a loss. Whether the loss is a friendship, a spouse, a wayward teenager, or something else emotionally devastating, they must mourn it. Something that could, should, or ought to have been will not be a part of their present reality.

Since their situation does not meet with the ideas they had regarding how things should be, they must move toward accepting reality. They need to allow others the freedom not to behave within this realm of expectations. After all, no one can control someone else's behavior.

People need to allow themselves to fail; after all, men and women are not perfect beings. This is not to say that in accepting the situation, one condones the negative behaviors of others or of oneself. But in accepting the reality of negative behavior, people open themselves to the ability of the Holy Spirit to perform a work of healing in their lives.

After accepting the situation as it actually is, people can then participate in their healing process by assuming the responsibility to better the situation. The Bible speaks of the work of the Holy Spirit in the life of the believer, but it never places the Christian in a passive role in the process of spiritual growth. We must be active participants.

We are not to let the preacher preach, the teacher teach, and the prayer committee pray for us without participating in personal devotion, Bible study, and prayer.

Too many people view God as a divine errand boy. This view is backward. God does not serve us; we serve Him. Participating in our recovery is in reality a part of service to God. Occasionally, I get a client who wants God to zap his situation back to the way it ought to be. But it is through the process of suffering that the Holy Spirit is able to convict our wrong, heal our pain, and strengthen our walk.

Christ came that we might have life and have it more abundantly. Knowing this gives us the ability to anticipate a change in our situation. It enables us to know that the emotional pain will last only a little while. Then it, too, will pass away. God is with us; He will not leave nor forsake us (Hebrews 13:5). According to Romans 8, He is working all things together for the good of those who love Him and are called according to His purpose. In the words of a song by Becky Fender, "God's got it all in control." As believers, we can know that there is health and healing in the name of Jesus Christ. Therefore, we can enthusiastically anticipate a change in our situation.

Finally, when we have received healing, we have the responsibility to attribute the victory to Christ. Through the act of giving Jesus Christ the credit for making our situation better, we do two things—we give God due glory, and we give other believers hope in the God of all comfort. God does hear and help us. Each of us needs to know that God is always with us. However, because people are human, they sometimes forget and become discouraged. Through our testimony, others receive strength to move forward in their quest for God's healing in their situation.

Also, this victory will give us confidence for the future. It may take awhile before there is deliverance, so believers need the witness of God's faithful and effective work through His Spirit.

Whether we experience a life of spiritual victory or defeat after our world shatters is up to us. Both options are available; the choice is ours. Figure 1 is a representation of the steps toward victory. Taking the steps on the path of health and healing is sure to bring victory. Yes, the scars of the past will still exist, but they will no longer be sensitive wounds or causes of present pain.

Figure 2 is a representation of what occurs in the life of a believer who chooses not to take God's direction. As you can see, the path is one of anger, bitterness, loneliness, depression, thoughts of suicide, and defeat. That is not what God wants for His children. He wants us to experience triumph over sin and its negative impact in our lives. He wants all believers to be able to say, with our brother, the apostle Paul, "But thanks be to God! He gives us the victory through our Lord Jesus Christ" (1 Corinthians 15:57).

Figure 1: Choosing to Confront Our Problems

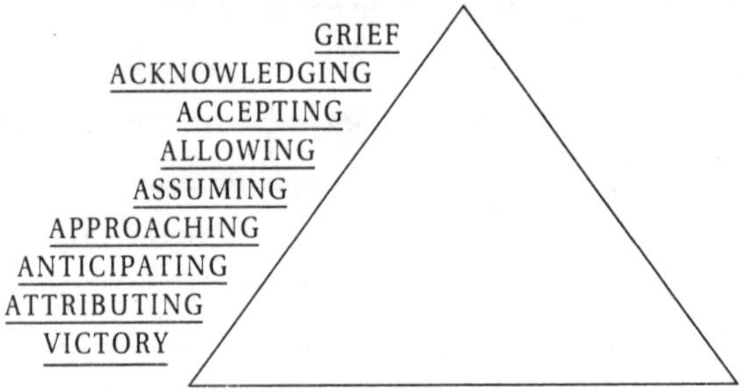

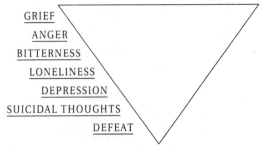

Figure 2: Choosing NOT to Confront Our Problems

Eleven

Maintaining
Our Repaired World

The journey toward repairing your shattered world may take you over a rough road. It is not easy to put the pieces back together. Repairing your life and relationships will warrant a great deal of patience and spiritual strength. Once you have repaired the damage, you will want to maintain the state of health. The only way to keep a building clean and in good condition is to follow a regular maintenance schedule.

When I first came to the United States, I was surprised to see how much schools and corporations spend on building maintenance. I once had a job with the maintenance crew in my school and couldn't understand why the school would pay me and hundreds of others thousands of dollars to clean the building every day. I came from a culture where companies, schools, or individuals don't spend a lot of money or contract work out with maintenance companies. People from my culture will erect buildings that are worth millions but will have no plan for maintenance. Of course, buildings not maintained will deteriorate eventually.

It is not enough just to have a maintenance schedule. You must follow it. You will need motivation, a plan, and follow-through.

Without all three, one should not expect to maintain what was achieved through prayerful effort.

Paul wrote to the Galatian church to urge them to give up on the idea of earning favor from the Lord through works. Through the preaching of the Gospel, Paul had previously announced that they were freed from trying to appease God by keeping regulations. Their life in Christ had given them a fresh, new start. However, some of them were about to turn and go back to those old destructive patterns.

I'm sure Paul would give those of you who are wounded today the same advice. Flee from the things that caused and maintained your brokenness. Avoid those things that do not profit you in your quest for righteousness. Align yourself to principles that will help you to maintain healthy relationships and to continue the process of repair in other relationships. The first step toward maintaining our repaired world is to develop a thriving relationship with God.

A Thriving Relationship with God

More than anything, God desires for us to have a thriving relationship with Him. By doing so, we can comprehend and achieve true fulfillment. Many people attempt to substitute religious service for a relationship with the Father; however, neither church attendance nor religious service can compensate for a lack of fellowship with God.

The apostle Paul expressed the priority of fellowship with God in this manner: "What is more, I consider everything a loss compared to the surpassing greatness of knowing Christ Jesus my Lord, for whose sake I have lost all things. I consider them rubbish, that I may gain Christ" (Philippians 3:8). Paul uttered these words just after divulging the value he placed in his religious service. Before his conversion, Paul placed stock in his status in life and his accomplishments: "Circumcised on the eighth day, of the people of Israel, of the tribe of Benjamin, a Hebrew of Hebrews; in regard to the law, a Pharisee; as for zeal, persecuting the church; as for legalistic right-eousness, faultless. But whatever was to my profit I now consider loss for the sake of Christ" (Philippians 3:5-7).

All other pursuits in life must give way to the necessity of loving the Father in heaven. That God wants to have a personal relationship with us rings loudly throughout the Scriptures. What is even more important is the type of relationship God wants with us. Romans 8:14-15 tells us that we are to consider ourselves the sons and daughters of God by virtue of adoption through Christ. Our adoption gives us the right to call God "Abba." *Abba*, an Aramaic word, roughly translates into English as "Daddy." God welcomes us as His own children. We belong to a divine family.

The fatherhood of God provides many, if not all, Christians an opportunity to be parented in the correct way. As I discussed earlier, many Christians suffer fallout from negative parenting techniques. Earthly parents, no matter how good, cannot compare to God. He is not only "Father of the Year," but He is also the "Father of Eternity." What earthly father can provide salvation for your soul as well as power and grace for your everyday life? God accomplished all these things in spite of our lack of appreciation and love for Him. "For if, when we were God's enemies, we were reconciled to him through the death of his Son, how much more, having been reconciled, shall we be saved through his life" (Romans 5:10).

Justification was just the beginning of God's provision of an abundant life for us. A whole world of new opportunity lies before us because Christ now lives again, and He lives for our benefit in the same manner that He died for our benefit.

We have so many things for which to be thankful. Even if pres-sures and painful circumstances press against us so as to crush us, we need not fear. There is One in heaven who desires to see that we become whole and healthy, but our trek to spiritual health requires that we seek Him first. God is the place of safety, assurance, and refuge for all who believe in Him. Psalm 91:1-3 says, "He who dwells in the shelter of the Most High will rest in the shadow of the Almighty. I will say of the LORD, 'He is my refuge and my fortress, my God, in whom I trust.' Surely he will save you from the fowler's snare and from the deadly pestilence." Begin today seeking God as your refuge. Pray and ask the Lord for love, obedience, and a heart for service—all for Him.

Love for God is the place of beginning to understand Him truly. Through love for God, service and obedience become relevant. Jesus stated that the greatest of all the commandments is: "Love the Lord your God with all your heart and with all your soul and with all your mind" (Matthew 22:37). Only within the venue of love for the Lord can the rest of Christian service and the Christian life make sense.

Biblical Instruction

Without Bible study, growing in the faith is next to impossible. In the Bible, we learn who God is and what He expects from us. We learn about the benefits that accrue to us through life in the Son. The Bible teaches about our access to and identity with Christ. This sense of identity is the basis for all endeavors in our lives, whether the endeavors are victorious or not.

The notion of identification with Christ saturates the New Testament. The Christian is identified with the death of Christ and the life of Christ. In the Great Commission, Christ gives the command to identify the future believers as Trinitarians. The Greek word *baptizo* in Matthew 28:19 signifies more than just immersion in water. *Baptizo* advances the idea of identification. In the early church, the rite of baptism signified that a person wished to be affiliated with those who trusted Jesus Christ.

The concept of identification is particularly important to saints with shattered lives. When believers comprehend their new position in Christ, they begin to live in a new way. They "put on" (practice) Christlike behaviors. The old carnal behaviors pass away as believers put these to death and resist them. Their new life in Christ is constituted differently from their former manner of life. Many of the epistles in the New Testament were written for the very purpose of reestablishing this identification between the saints of the first century and their resurrected Lord (Galatians 5; Colossians 3:1-4; Philippians 3). Often Paul evangelized new believers, only to have some of them fall away through temptation. The sinful behavior that followed bore no resemblance to the behavior required in the teachings of Christ. A healthy Christian life will, to say the least, require Bible study. Few things contribute more to a profitable Christian life than the study of Scripture (2 Timothy 3:16).

Discipleship

The word *discipleship* does not occur in the New Testament; however, the concept of discipleship is certainly taught there. This notion of discipleship is pertinent to the Christian faith because it insures that successive generations of Christians will be properly trained in the rule and practice of the faith. Discipleship also provides a forum where young developing Christians may see the power of a Christ-centered life. There is no substitute for relating. After all, relating is essential to our very being.

The word used throughout the Gospels and Acts for disciple is *mathetes*. It refers to a variety of people—some positive examples of a disciple and some not. In some instances, it speaks of those who merely follow Jesus. This practice continues today. Every Sunday at 11:00 A.M., people all over the country file into church to participate in worship services, but they have no real concept of who God is. They are just there.

In other places in Scripture, the word *mathetes* refers only to the twelve men Jesus selected to travel with Him. Passages such as Matthew 14:15 discriminate between those who were Jesus' disciples and the throng of people who simply followed Him: "As evening approached, the disciples came to him and said, 'This is a remote place, and it's already getting late. Send the crowds away, so they can go to the villages and buy themselves some food.'" John 6:53 was a very direct saying used by Christ to distill the true believers from among the general populace: "Jesus said to them, 'I tell you the truth, unless you eat the flesh of the Son of Man and drink his blood, you have no life in you. Whoever eats my flesh and drinks my blood has eternal life, and I will raise him up at the last day. For my flesh is real food and my blood is real drink. Whoever eats my flesh and drinks my blood remains in me, and I in him.'"

John 6:66 revealed the fallout of this "hard saying": "From this time many of his disciples turned back and no longer followed him." One might conclude from this episode that a true disciple has spiritual insight into difficult, or seemingly difficult, requirements of the faith. This does not mean that a true disciple will understand everything said to him, but rather that difficult truths will not sway his allegiance. All those who were called by the name *mathetes* were not necessarily true followers. So then discipleship is not simply a matter of religious affiliation. In its truest meaning, it refers to one who follows for the sake of learning from a mentor.

There is, however, an essential that cannot be overlooked. There is a calling from Jesus and a correct response to it. Discipleship must begin with this elemental principle. Commitment and conviction on the part of the disciple are requirements. This does not mean that a disciple will walk flawlessly, but it does imply that his or her walk is intended to please God.

For all that discipleship is, it requires a lot of on-the-job training. The lessons are communicated using everyday life as the setting. This was certainly the case for Christ and His disciples. The Lord used various settings for background and context to instruct the disciples in the way of the kingdom. Situations such as the feeding of the 5,000 (John 6:1-71) left an indelible impression on the minds of the disciples. Christians today also need this hands-on kind of training.

Character Qualities

The common denominator for all Christians will be faith in Christ. This is an all-consuming quality that should permeate every area of life, especially counteracting those sinful exits that take us away from fulfillment with God. Faith not only brings the disciple into Christianity, but faith also is the energy God provides for the disciple to live a life "worthy of the calling to which he has been called" (Ephesians 4:1). This is the *sine qua non*, or essence, of discipleship, without respect to the disciple's tenure of experience in the faith. Scripture describes the traits of a disciple that Jesus deemed paramount.

Obedience is the supreme character trait that Jesus Himself placed before men as an acid test to see if they were true disciples or simply "loitering-around holy people." John 8:31-32 says, "If you hold to my teaching, you are really my disciples. Then you will know the truth and the truth will set you free." Acknowledgment of the Christ via obedience to His teachings culminates in freedom from sin.

Another prominent trait of a disciple of Christ is love. Again these are the words of the Savior: "A new command I give you: Love one another. As I have loved you, so you must love one another. By this all men will know that you are my disciples, if you love one another" (John 13:34-35). Love is at the core of the mission of Christ (John 3:16). Therefore, it would be inconceivable that He would omit this most crucial element in His definition of a disciple. It is by this very love, with its unique character and action, exhibited among His followers that nonbelievers could identify those who follow the Lord Jesus Christ. Paul certainly did his best to demonstrate the superiority of love above all other virtues, gifts, and talents. A life that is not informed by love is not informed by God.

Servanthood is another critical trait that emerges from the gospel of Mark. Specifically, Mark 10:45 provides us with the ultimate paradigm for discipleship: "For even the Son of Man did not come to be served, but to serve, and to give his life as a ransom for many." The evangelist Mark uses considerable space to give his readers this profile of Christ as the consummate servant.

Another trait of a disciple is eagerness to glorify God through the spiritual fruit he or she bears. "This is to my Father's glory, that you bear much fruit, showing yourselves to be my disciples" (John 15:8). One's identity as a Christian should be a loud and boisterous announcement even without a single word being spoken. A changed life, both inwardly and outwardly, subjectively and objectively, should be the mark of a disciple. The outward behavior exposes the depth of commitment created by the inner reality of the presence of God in the life of the disciple through the indwelling Holy Spirit.

Luke 14:26-27 teaches that discipleship is not without its cost: "If anyone comes to me and does not hate his father and mother, his wife and children, his brothers and sisters—yes, even his own life— he cannot be my disciple. And anyone who does not carry his cross and follow me cannot be my disciple." Certainly, this verse does not sound like a spot advertisement for "Focus on the Family." The one who bore the cross bore it with condemnation, scorn, and ridicule from this world.

One should not gather from Jesus' statement that He is anti-family. What one is to understand is that discipleship demands unparalleled allegiance to Christ. Christ is to be the supreme authority and concern of the Christian's life. This not only includes prioritizing Him above family but above everything else in life. "In the same way, any of you who does not give up everything he has cannot be my disciple" (Luke 14:33). This preoccupation with giving everything to Christ should not be viewed as though it were a compulsive addiction. Christ does not consume our lives to destroy them; rather, He builds us up in every area of life for excellence. We have much to gain in return for our complete allegiance. Christ will change our lives and our minds to focus on living righteously rather than on wallowing in the repulsive habits of our past.

Life Changes

Life changes are not optional. Life as a disciple of Christ requires that we alter the state of our lives, and the process of change will not always be comfortable. But even though we suffer through the process of changing unseemly aspects of our lives, there is much to gain from the experience of trusting Christ throughout all of our lifetime.

John's categories of discipleship are clear with respect to this notion of a changed life. The call to discipleship warrants behavioral modifications; however, these modifications are to be conditioned by a change in character. The character of the disciple undergoes a shift, a reorientation to a renewed life in Christ Jesus. What changes is his or her spiritual perception: "I pray also that the eyes of your heart may be enlightened in order that you may know the hope to which he has called you, the riches of his glorious inheritance in the saints, and his incomparably great power for us who believe. That power is like the working of his mighty strength" (Ephesians 1:18-19).

Within the context of any discipling scenario, there must be a focus on development in both life patterns (habits) and in doctrine. This cannot be an either/or proposition. It is correct doctrine that prevents slipping into potentially destructive patterns of living and thinking (Ephesians 4:14).

Strategy for Implementation

Discipleship needs to be a movement within the church and not a gimmick or strategy of church polity. Discipleship should not grow out of a church program. Church programs are typically impersonal and often do not include participation from the higher echelons of the church. The trend in modern ecclesiology is to hire someone out of seminary to do the work. Thus, the fervor of the pastor and his zeal and love for the Lord are not experienced by the congregation first-hand. His views on life and discipleship are spilled out from the pulpit or disseminated through hired hands to the church community at large. Many churches have gone from "equipping the saints to do the work of the ministry" to "equipping the saints to pay for the work of the ministry" (Ephesians 4:12-13).

The notion of personal involvement dissipates when church leadership does not make itself available to the ordinary members. This is not to say that everyone in the congregation should be discipled by the pastor but that it should be evident to the congregation at large that the pastor is a co-laborer in the training process. The primary key to discipleship is relationships. Many ministries in this day and time seek to devise better programs, systems, and schemes to affect the lives of the members of the church. However, systems do not change people; mentoring under the direction of the Holy Spirit changes them.

The most integral factor in the process of discipleship is the relationship developed between the shepherd and the disciples. Imagine what would have happened if Jesus had simply yelled down instructions from heaven as opposed to appearing in the form of human flesh in order that men might understand Him and His mission. When the disciples of Jesus saw His obedience to the point of death on a cross, this must have made a huge impression on them. The mission of Christ and His investment in the disciples was a personal matter. It is only logical that discipleship models in the present day should follow this methodology that turned the world upside down with a paltry number of people.

Discipleship cannot be accomplished by remote control. Today many seek to do discipling from the pulpit. The pulpit, for all that it is, is not the best venue for communicating the principles of discipleship. What is lost is the impact provided through modeling. There is a great need in the church today for men and women who will devote themselves to discipling other people.

The first step in discipleship is to establish a relationship. This is the responsibility of the shepherd and not the disciple. It should come as no surprise that the Bible refers to the followers of Christ as "sheep." Sheep do very little to advance their own welfare. They will eat anything, even if it is not good for them. They will wander off. They will go into areas that are dangerous without regard to the peril that may come their way. But most of all, the sheep are not responsible for finding a shepherd for themselves. This is the shepherd's job.

The next step is to surround the disciple with an environment conducive to growth. This requires a number of things: (1) contextual Bible study, (2) relational prayer which includes confession, (3) relationships with other disciples in loving accountability, and (4) most importantly, a shepherd.

Goal: Targeting and Time Involvement

Discipleship is not a computerized process that feeds the disciple some information, and he spits up righteousness. Nor can it necessarily be a timed program where an individual spends thirty minutes in the field, and automatically he will come out with a bushel of peas. Discipleship is an ongoing concern with multiple stages. A disciple may grow to the point of having several pupils under him or her, yet still be in need of further training. There is no shame in this. One does not have to be a know-it-all to be a tangible influence in someone else's life.

But for the sake of benchmark figures, I think that the discipler should spend at least a period of three months with the disciple. Furthermore, during this three-month period, the discipler should seek to surround the disciple with an environment conducive to continued growth. Also, there should be adequate follow-up. The apostle Paul used letter-writing as a vehicle to encourage his protégés in the ministry. Reinforcement and motivation are certainly to govern the whole process of discipleship.

A good portion of this time should be geared toward dealing with the practical side of life as it intersects with Scripture. Thus, the venue of training should be outside of the local church edifice. If not, the Christian faith for the disciple may become restricted to what happens in church. Most of life happens away from the church building; so it would only seem fitting to do most of the training in the place where the disciple lives out his or her life. The objective is to make the Bible a living experience and not necessarily to create a biblical scholar. The goal is to "Go! make disciples . . . teaching them to obey all that I have commanded." The passage does not say, "Teach them Bible stuff." The love for knowledge in the American church is exceeded only by its intolerance for hypocrisy. True, knowledge and education are important, but they do not cover up a multitude of sins. Christ-centered friendships are to be desired above all else. It is this bond between two or more people that gives one individual access to another to question and reprove or encourage habits and modes of thinking. Friendship should be at the core of the endeavor of the shepherd. There is biblical attestation for this concept. "You are my friends if you do what I command. I no longer call you servants, because a servant does not know his master's business. Instead, I have called you friends, for everything that I learned from my Father I have made known to you" (John 15:14-15).

The disciple should also have the opportunity to watch the discipler train other Christians. This is significant because it shows the disciple how to continue the process of developing others for ministry as well.

Accountability

Accountability is an extremely critical aspect of maintaining one's state of repair. Accountability is more than just a word. It is in itself a facet of relationship. Accountability for the recovering saint must exist on at least two levels.

First, the recovered saint needs accountability with a counselor. The counselor, along with the help of other brothers and sisters in Christ, keeps the recovered one's focus on a godly and healthy life. Therapy is an ongoing process. The therapy of the Holy Spirit that leads us into sanctification is the most critical kind. The Spirit is the ultimate Counselor who is able to govern our conduct as we live out our faith. "So I say, live by the Spirit, and you will not gratify the desires of the sinful nature" (Galatians 5:16).

A human counselor is not, I repeat not, a substitute for the guidance of the Holy Spirit. The human counselor functions as a facilitator. He assists the growing Christian in understanding who and what he or she is in Christ relative to the dreadful habits of the old life. Counseling is not the renewal process; it is only an aspect of it. Nevertheless, counseling is extremely important to the individual prone to exit the ways and habits essential to the Christian faith. Whereas an individual may have trouble looking at his or her own life objectively, the counselor is able to view the overall trend of a person's life and observe traits and habits that may elude the counselee.

Second and most important of all, accountability must exist between the recovered believer and other mature believers. Believers who congregate and fellowship together are able to help and encourage one another. Access is the key notion here. One can in no way be accountable to other individuals if he or she is never around them. Isolation does not foster interpersonal growth. Isolation breeds despair, depression, and confusion. People who are depressed seldom are even able to pick themselves up by their boot straps or cheer themselves up. If anything has become clear from the pages of this book, it is that people need other people. God has designed all people for relationships. "No man is an island."

With the proper vision and equipping, the church can meet both the individual's need for counseling as well as the need for accountability after counseling has taken place. What better place is there than the local church to hold people accountable and encourage personal growth? Certainly, the fellowship of the redeemed must be a healing place where the Great Physician and those filled with His Spirit help the broken to find wholeness in Christ Jesus.

Suggested Resources

Allender, Dan B. *The Wounded Heart: Hope for Adult Victims of Childhood Sexual Abuse.* Colorado Springs: NavPress, 1990.

Christenson, Larry. *The Christian Family.* Minneapolis: Bethany Fellowship, 1970.

Cloud, Henry. *When Your World Makes No Sense.* Nashville: Oliver Nelson (Thomas Nelson), 1990.

Crabb, Lawrence. *The Marriage Builder.* Grand Rapids: Zondervan, 1982.

Flanders, Bill and Marianne. *God's Family Plan.* Kalamazoo: Master's Press, 1976.

Guernsey, Dennis. *Thoroughly Married.* Waco: Word, 1975.

Hendricks, Howard G. *Heaven Help the Home.* Wheaton, Ill.: Victor, 1973.

LaHaye, Tim. *What Everyone Should Know About Homosexuality.* Wheaton, Ill.: Living Books (Tyndale), 1978.

Lewis, Margie M. *The Hurting Parent.* Grand Rapids: Zondervan, 1976.

Lutzer, Erwin. *Managing Your Emotions.* Wheaton, Ill.: Victor, 1983.

MacArthur, John, Jr. *The Family.* Chicago: Moody, 1982.

MacDonald, Gordon. *Magnificent Marriage.* Wheaton, Ill.: Living Books (Tyndale), 1976.

Martin, Grant L. *Counseling for Family Violence and Abuse.* Waco: Word, 1987.

McDowell, Josh. *Givers, Takers & Other Kinds of Lovers.* Wheaton, Ill.: Living Books (Tyndale), 1980.

McGee, Springle, and Craddock. *Your Parents and You.* Waco: Word/Rapha, 1990.

_____. *Search for Significance.* Waco: Word/Rapha, 1990.

Meier, Paul D., Frank B. Minirth and Frank B. Wichern. *Introduction to Psychology and Counseling.* Grand Rapids: Baker, 1982.

Minirth, Frank B. and Paul D. Meier. *Happiness Is a Choice.* Grand Rapids: Baker, 1978.

Narramore, Clyde. *The Psychology of Counseling.* Grand Rapids: Zondervan, 1960.

Payne, Leanne. *The Healing of the Homosexual.* Wheaton, Ill.: Crossway Books, 1984.

Rainey, Dennis and Barbara. *Building Your Mate's Self-Esteem.* San Bernardino: Here's Life Publishers, 1986.

Seamands, David A. *Healing for Damaged Emotions.* Wheaton, Ill.: Victor, 1981.

Smedes, Lewis B. *Forgive and Forget.* New York: Harper & Row, 1984.

Springle, Pat. *Co-dependency.* Houston: Word/Rapha, 1990.

Swindoll, Chuck. *For Those Who Hurt.* Portland, Ore.: Multnomah, 1977.

_____. *Starting Over.* Portland, Ore.: Multnomah, 1977.

White, John. *Parents in Pain.* Downers Grove, Ill.: InterVarsity Press, 1979.

Wright, H. Norman. *Communication: Key to Your Marriage.* Ventura: Regal, 1974.

Walvoord, John E., ed. *Christian Counseling for Contemporary Problems.* Dallas: Dallas Theological Seminary, Christian Education Department, 1968.

General Index

Scripture Index